I0400887

حكي كل يوم

2

Haki Kill Yoom

Situational Levantine Arabic

Rita Housseiny
Alaa Abou El Nour
Matthew Aldrich

lingualism

ISBN: 978-1-949650-07-5

Written by Rita Housseiny, Alaa Abou El Nour, and Matthew Aldrich
Edited by Nadine-Lama Choucaire and Matthew Aldrich
Illustrated by Heba Khater
Audio by Nadine-Lama Choucaire, Dayana Choucaire, and Mohammed Ellaz
Cover art: photo: © iStockphoto/ marcociannarel; illustration: Heba Khater

website: www.lingualism.com
email: contact@lingualism.com

Table of Contents

Table of Contents .... *i*
Introduction .... *ii*
How to Use This Book .... *iv*
At the Supermarket 1
At the Butcher's 15
In a Clothing Shop 29
At the Market 45
At a Hotel 59
Renting an Apartment 73
Dealing with a Housekeeper 89
Laundry and Tailoring 103
At the Post Office 117
At the Bank 130
Visiting a Museum 144
At a Mosque 157
At a Church 173
Dealing with the Police 186
Dealing with Difficulties 199

Introduction

Haki Kill Yoom: Situational Levantine Arabic was written to help intermediate learners succeed at critical moments during everyday communicative tasks.

This is the second of two books in a series. Each book has been divided into 15 chapters, which are not meant to be studied in order and do not increase in the level of difficulty. Instead, you should find the chapter to navigate your way through a particular transactional or social situation that is relevant to your needs.

Learning natural, idiomatic phrasing and vocabulary is essential to both listening and speaking, not only for living in Lebanon or another Levantine Arabic speaking country, but also for communicating in Arabic with immigrants in your own country.

Each chapter has several dialogues, vocabulary lists, bonus expressions, footnotes, and cultural information. (See How to Use This Book on page iv to learn more about the organization and features of the chapters.)

Levantine Arabic is the umbrella term for a number of closely related and mutually intelligible dialects in the Levant (Lebanon, Syria, Jordan, and Palestine). Beiruti Lebanese, specifically, is the variety featured in Haki Kill Yoom. That said, you should find it easy to communicate with people throughout the region using what you learn from this book. Of course, there may be subtle differences in pronunciation, vocabulary, and even grammar, but these you can note, as needed, when dealing with speakers from other parts of the Levant to hone your style to match theirs, if that is your goal.

I would like to thank Rita Housseiny for adapting the original dialogues (written by Alaa Abou El Nour) to reflect authentic, everyday Levantine Arabic and for adding original dialogues and cultural notes to include high-frequency vocabulary and phrases likely to be heard and used in specific situations. I would also like to thank Nadine-Lama Choucaire for her help proofreading and editing the dialogues and vocabulary lists. Special thanks also to Heba Khater for providing illustrations and to Nadine-Lama Choucaire, Dayana Choucaire, and Mohammed Ellaz for recording the accompanying audio.

Matthew Aldrich

Audio

Visit www.lingualism.com/audio, where you can find the free accompanying audio to download or stream (at variable playback rates).

Anki Flashcards

Enhance your learning with our Anki digital flashcards, available for separate purchase on our website. This comprehensive deck features all the vocabulary and expressions from this book, complete with audio, to help you memorize and master the material more effectively.

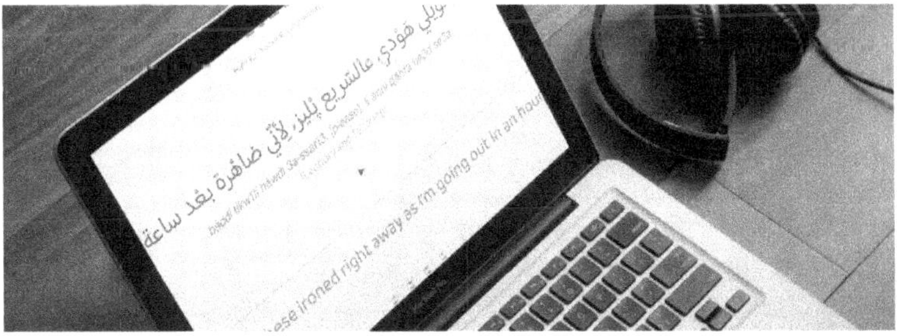

How to Use This Book

This is not a coursebook with chapters that build on each other and need to be studied in order. Use the **Table of Contents** at the front of the book (also located on the back cover of the paperback edition, for your convenience) to find the topic that interests you for your immediate or future communicative goals. Of course, you're not going to go out into the real world and have conversations with people that follow the dialogues line by line. The purpose of the dialogues is to teach you different words and phrases that you can use and that you may hear. Synonyms, alternative expressions, and supplementary vocabulary are provided to help you form your own sentences to express yourself and to be prepared for the variety of possible things you may hear people say to you.

Introductory Paragraph

On the first page of each chapter, you will see an illustration above the chapter's title in English and Levantine Arabic. An introduction to the topic follows and often presents key vocabulary.

Mini-Dialogues

Next, we have several short dialogues. Each dialogue has a title that shows you the goal of the specific "subtask"–for example, paying the bill, offering your seat to someone, reporting a theft.

Symbols

Notice that the lines of dialogue are preceded by symbols.

○ You–the foreigner, the customer. (Things you might need to say.)

◇ A local–merchant, barber, waiter, landlord, friend, etc. etc. (Things you might hear other people say.)

The symbols are there to help you decide whether you need to memorize the phrases so you can actively use them yourself, or if you just need to be able to passively understand them when you hear them.

Arabic Script

Each dialogue appears three times on the page. The first is written in Arabic script with tashkeel (diacritics). At first glance, it may seem that many letters are missing diacritics. A final consonant is assumed to take sukuun, as Levantine Arabic does not have case endings as MSA does.

We write كْتاب *ktēb* **book** (and not كْتَابْ). Non-final consonants without diacritics are understood to take the short vowel fatha (َ): مكْتب *máktab* **desk** (and not مَكْتَبْ). This was done intentionally to keep the texts from being cluttered with redundancies and streamline fluent reading. You can find a detailed online guide on Levantine Arabic pronunciation and Lingualism's system of orthography in the Resources section of this book's product page on our website.

Phonemic Transcription

Each dialogue also appears as phonemic transcription. This can be helpful for learners who are not yet comfortable enough with the Arabic alphabet. Some of the phonemic characters may seem unfamiliar and confusing, but by investing just a short time learning the sounds each character represents, you will find the system intuitive and easy to read. The phonemic transcription shows some pronunciation information, such as word stress, that the Arabic script does not. So even learners who prefer Arabic script can benefit by referring to the phonemic transcription. Words borrowed from English (and pronounced, more or less, as in English) are shown between [square brackets]. French words are, also shown in square brackets and preceded by a superscript ^{F}. Follow the link above for a guide to Lingualism's phonemic transcription system.

English Translation

Between the dialogues of Arabic script and phonemic transcription, English translations appear to help you understand the dialogues and quickly find words and phrases you want to learn. Some style was sacrificed in the translations to keep them direct and true to the original Levantine Arabic. This allows you to easily match up phrases and words by comparing the translations to the Arabic.

Footnotes

Underlined words and phrases are followed by superscript numbers that reference footnotes. When an entire line of dialogue is referenced, it is not underlined.:

- Synonyms are preceded by equal signs (=). These show you words and expressions which can replace those in the dialogue without significantly changing the meaning.

- Alternative expressions show examples of other things you might want to say or might hear instead. These are followed by English translations.

Culture and Information Notes

The real focus of the book is, of course, the language itself. Other information–on culture and services in Lebanon–is provided as a bonus. Hopefully, you will find some information useful and interesting, but keep in mind that the comments on culture are generalizations–there are always exceptions. Likewise, the information on services (companies, procedures, transportation options, etc.) is subject to change. You should always double-check such information from other sources, especially Lebanese friends and acquaintances.

The Extended Dialogue

The mini-dialogues in each chapter are followed by a longer dialogue that combines several of the subtasks into a full communicative exchange.

Vocabulary

Vocabulary lists in three columns (English, phonemic transcription, and Arabic script) follow the dialogues. These are not glossaries containing all of the words from the dialogues, but rather lists of keywords related to the topic and those likely to be needed in various circumstances–that is, they are there to save you time searching in dictionaries for words you might need.

Expressions

Expressions are divided into two sections, preceded by the same symbols used in the dialogues. First are expressions you may need to use, and second are statements and questions you may hear others say.

Audio

All of the dialogues have been recorded by native-speaker voice artists. You can download or stream the audio free of charge from our website.

At the Supermarket بِالسّوبِرْمارْكِت

A سوپِرْمارْكِت *[supermarket]* **supermarket** in Lebanon is a big deal. It has everything from vegetables to toiletries, and it is where Lebanese often do their monthly grocery shopping. Mega stores (equivalent to Wallmart or Target) are called هَيْپِرْمارْكِت *[hypermarket].* Supermarkets are often very crowded on weekends and evenings, especially since going to the supermarket is, in some parts of Lebanon, a family affair. Normally, if you want to buy just a couple of things, you would avoid the supermarkets and go to a دِكّان *dikkēn* (which is a small, corner store that has the basics: some groceries, fruit and vegetables, snacks, sodas, small packs of toilet paper, etc.) or a ميني مارْكِت *[minimarket].*

IN THE PRODUCE DEPARTMENT (1)

o هَوْدي المنْجا بِالكيلو أَوْ بِالقِطْعة؟[1]
◇ بِالكيلو. الكيلو سِتّلاف. بسّ فيكي تْنقّيْن عَ ذَوْقِك.
o أوْكي. زِنْلي هَوْدي التّنْيْن پْليز.
◇ هَوْدي تْلات رْباع الكيلو. مِنْزيد[2] هَيْدي الزّْغيرِة ومْنعْمِلْن كيلو؟
o أوْكي[3]، ما في مشْكل.

o Are these mangoes sold by the kilo or by the piece?
◇ By the kilo. The kilo for 6,000 L.L. You can pick them out yourself.
o Okay. Weigh these two mangoes for me.
◇ They weigh three-quarters of a kilo. Shall we add this small one to them to make an even kilo?
o All right, no problem.

o *háwdi -lmánga bi-lkīlu aw bi-lʔíṭ3a?*[1]
◇ *bi-lkīlu. -lkīlu sittalēf. bass fīki tnaʔʔíyun 3a záwʔik.*
o *okē. zínli háwdi -ttnēn, [please].*
◇ *háwdi tlēt rbē3 ilkīlu. minzīd*[2] *háydi -zzɣīri w mná3milun kīlu?*
o *okē*[3]*, ma fī máškal.*

[1] كيف عم تْبيعوهُن؟ *kīf 3am tbī3ūhun?* **How are they sold?** (lit. How do you sell them?)

[2] = مِنْضيف *minḍīf*

[3] = طيِّب *ṭáyyib*

2

In the Produce Department (2)

○ الخْيارات طازة؟
◇ أكيد مدام. هلّق وِصْلوا مْن شْوَيّ.
○ أوْكي، عْطيني كيس پْليز، تنقّي اللي بدّي ياهُن.
◇ تْفضّلي، المحلّ كِلّو عَ حْسابِك.
○ مرْسي! زِنْلي[1] هَوْدي پْليز وقِلّي قدّيْ بْيِطْلعوا.
◇ زيدي بعْد وِحْدِة تَيْصيروا كيلو عالقدّ.

○ Are the cucumbers fresh?
◇ Of course, they are, ma'am. They just came in a little while ago.
○ Okay, hand me a plastic bag, please, so I can pick the ones I want.
◇ Here you are. The entire shop is at your service.
○ Thank you! Weigh these for me and let me know how much they come out to.
◇ Add one more to make an even kilo.

○ *lixyārāt ţāza?*
◇ *akīd, [Fmadame]. hálla? wíşlu mn šwayy.*
○ *okē, 3ţīni kīs [please], ta-ná??i -lli báddi yēhun.*
◇ *tfáḑḑali, -lmaħáll kíllu 3a ħsēbik.*
○ *[Fmerci]! zínli[1] háwdi [please] w ?ílli ?addē byíţla3u.*
◇ *zīdi ba3d wíħdi ta-yşīru kīlu 3a-l?ádd.*

[1] زان (يْزين) *zēn (yzīn)* **to weigh**

3

In the dairy department

○ عِنْدك لبْنِة بلدية؟

◇ أيْه مدام. مِنْجيب اللّبْنِة مِن مزْرعة مْرتّبِة مْن اللّقْلوق.

○ عظيم، فِيي آخُد تْنيْن كيلو، پْليز؟[1]

◇ أكيد، بِتْحِبّي شي تاني؟[2]

○ باخُد تْلات مية غْرام حلّوم، ووْقِيِّة عكّاوي.[3]

◇ تِكْرم عَيْنِك.[4]

○ Do you have organic, local labneh?

◇ Yes, ma'am. We get our labneh from a respected farm in Laklouk.

○ Great. Can I have two kilos, please?

◇ Sure! Anything else?

○ I'll take 300 grams of Halloumi cheese and an "ounce" of Akkawi cheese.

◇ You got it.

○ *3índak lábni baladíyyi?*

◇ *ē, [Fmadame]. minjīb illábni min mázra3a mráttabi mn illaʔlūʔ.*

○ *3aẓīm, fíyi ēxud tnēn kīlu, [please]?*[1]

◇ *akīd, bitḩíbbi šī tēni?*[2]

○ *bēxud tlēt mīt grām ḩallūm, w wʔíyyit 3akkēwi.*[3]

◇ *tíkram 3áynik.*[4]

[1] = طيِّب تعْطيني سطِل عْموْل معْروف؟ *ṭáyyib, ta3ṭīni sáṭil, 3mōl ma3rūf?* **Okay, can you give me a tub [of labneh], please?**

[2] = عايْزِة غيْر شي؟ *3āyzi ɣēr šī?*

[3] لأ يِسْلمو، عزّبْتك معي. *laʔ, yíslamu, 3azzábtak má3i.* **No, thanks. I've bothered you enough.** (This expression can be used after somone does a service for you, usually one requiring physical effort, such as handling bags, going from aisle to aisle getting you a product, etc.)

[4] = مِن عْيوني *min 3yūni*

4

In the Meat Department

o صباح الخيرْ، بدّي كفْته، پْليز. بسّ بسّ[1] إذا طازة.

◇ أيْه مدام. عِنّا لحْمِة بِتْجنِّن إجِت الصُّبْح. قدّيْ بِتْحِبّي أعْطيكي؟

o بسّ كيلو واحد. فِيي كمان آخُد كِبِّة؟

◇ أيْه أكيد، بِتْحِبّي تبِّلّك ياهُن[2]؟

o أيْه، پْليز، بدّي كِلّ شي عليُّن.

◇ تمام يَلّا ثَواني.

o Good morning, I'd like some kofta, please, but only if they're fresh.

◇ Yes, ma'am. We have some great meat that came in just this morning. How much would you like?

o Just one kilo, please. Can I also have kibbeh?

◇ Sure, of course. Would you like it seasoned?

o Yes, please. All the works.

◇ Great, coming right up.

o *ṣabāḫ ilxēr, báddi káfta, [please]. bass báss[1] íza ṭāza.*

◇ *ē, [Fmadame]. 3ínna láḫmi bitjánnin íjit iṣṣúbuḫ. ʔaddē bitḫíbbi a3ṭīki?*

o *bass kīlu wāḫad. fíyi kamēn ēxud kíbbi?*

◇ *ē, akīd, bitḫíbbi tabbíllik yēhun[2]?*

o *ē, [please], báddi kill šī 3aláyyun.*

◇ *tamēm, yálla sawēni.*

[1] بسّ *bass* has two meanings, both of which we see here, as the conjunction **but** and the adverb **only**. Notice the emphasis on the second word in the audio.

[2] = ملِّحْن وبهِّرْن *mállíḫun w báhhirun* **salt and season them**

5

Asking where something is

- ○ عفواً، وِيْن فِيي لاقي معْجون سْنان؟
- ◇ معاجين السّْنان وفراشي السّْنان وَرا، رايوْن تمْانْتعْش بِفْتِكِر، دِغْري حدّ رايوْن وَرق التّْواليْت.
- ○ مرْسي! والدِيوْدوْران؟
- ◇ حدّ هَوْديك، رايوْن عِشْرين.
- ○ أوْكيْ، مرْسي كْتير.

- ○ Excuse me, where can I find toothpaste?
- ◇ The toothpaste and toothbrushes are in the back, aisle 18, I believe, right next to the toilet paper aisle.
- ○ Thanks! And the deodorant?
- ◇ Around there, as well. Aisle 20.
- ○ Okay, thank you so much!

- ○ *3áfwan, wēn fíyi lēʔi ma3jūn snēn?*
- ◇ *ma3ājīn issnēn w farāši -ssnēn wára, [Frayon] tmínta3š bíftikir, díɣri ɧadd [Frayon] wáraʔ it[Ftoilette].*
- ○ *[Fmerci]! w il[Fdéodorant]?*
- ◇ *ɧadd hawdīk, [Frayon] 3išrīn.*
- ○ *okē, [Fmerci] ktīr.*

6

Buying phone cards and lotto tickets

o لَوْ سمحِت، بِتْبيعوا شي كْروتِة تِشْريج للتِّلِفونْ[1]؟
◇ أيْه، بسّ هلّق خالْصين.[2]
o اه أوْكي، دوْماج. طيِّب[3]، عِنْدْكُن لوْتوْ شي؟
◇ أيْه عِنّا، كم وَرْقة بِتْحِبّ؟[4]
o وَرْقة وِحْدِة. فيك تعْطيني زيد[5] كمان پْليز؟
◇ أيْه، أكيد.

o Excuse me, do you sell prepaid phone cards here?
◇ Yes, we do, but we're out now.
o Oh, okay, that's a shame. Do you have lotto?
◇ Yes, we do. How many sheets would you like?
o Just one. Can you also give me a Zeed, please?
◇ Sure, of course.

o *law samáħit, bitbī3u šī krūtit tišrīj la-t[ᶠtéléphone][1]?*
◇ *ē, bass hálla? xālṣīn.[2]*
o *āh okē, [ᶠdommage].[3] táyyib, 3índkun [ᶠloto] šī?*
◇ *ē, 3ínna, kam wárʔa bitħíbb?[4]*
o *wárʔa wíħdi. fīk ta3ṭīni zīd[5] kamēn, [please]?*
◇ *ē, akīd.*

[1] تِشْريج *tišrīj* is derviced from the verb شرّج *šárraj* (from the English charge). كارْت تِشْريج *[ᶠcarte] tišrīj* is a prepaid card to load credit to your cell phone in Lebanon. There are two phone providers in Lebanon: Alfa and Touch (formerly known as MTC, and still often referred to by that name). / [2] تبع القدّيْ؟ *tába3 ilʔaddē?* **For how much?** (prepaid phone cards are available in varying amounts) / [3] عْطيني تبع العِشْرين. *3ṭīni tába3 il3išrīn.* **Give me the $20 one.** (the card with $20 in credits) / [4] كمْ شبكةِ حابّة تِقْطعي؟ *kam šábaki ħābbi tiʔṭá3i* **How many grids would you like to play?** / [5] زيد *zīd* **Zeed** is an additional game played on the Loto grid. www.lldj.com/en/DrawGames/Zeed/About

○ صباحو! وَلا مرّة جيت عَ هَيْدي السّوپِرْمارْكِت قبِل[1]، وبدّي شْوَيِّة مْساعدِة.

◇ صباحو دْمْوازيْل. وَلا يْهِمِّك أبداً. أنا بْساعْدِك. كيف فِيي ساعْدِك[2]؟

○ أوّل شي بدّي أعْرِف وِيْن قِسْم اللّحْمِة والجِبْنِة.

◇ هوْن، خلّينا نمِْشي سَوى.

(They walk over to the meat department.)

○ بوْنْجور مْعلّم، پْليز فِيي آخُد كيلو لحْمِة بقر للشّوي؟

◇ شي تاني؟

○ أيْه، بدّي تْنين كيلو مقانِق.

◇ حظِّك حِلو، إجانا مقانِق غيرْ شِكْل[3] اليوْم الصُّبْح.

○ تمام، قدّيْ بدّك منّي؟

◇ بْسعِّرْلِك ياهُن هوْن، بسّ فيكي تِدْفعي عالصّنْدوق بسّ تْخلّْصي كِلّ غْراضِك.

○ تمام، مرْسي.

(She looks at the clerk assisting her.)

○ أوْكيْ، بِفْتكِر رح جيب الجِبْنِة بعْديْن. رح جيب الإشْيا الضّرورية هلّق. ويْن فِيي لاقي لبْنِة.

◇ عِنْدِك اِحْتِماليْن: إمّا بْتاخْدِيا مِن قِسْم الجِبْنِة، فِليت[4] وبيوَضْبولِك ياها هونيك دغري. هَوْدي إجْمالاً بيكونوا طازة أكْتر، أَوْ فيكي تاخْدي يَلّي مْوَضّبين بِالبرّاد هونيك.

○ أوْكيْ، خلّينا نْروح عَ برّاد الجِبْنِة فإذاً، وهيْك بْجيب جِبْنِة ولبْنِة فرْد مرّة.

(They walk over to the cheese section.)

◇ أهْلا مدام، شو فِيي أعْطيكي؟

o فِي پْليز آخُد كيلو عكّاوي وتنين كيلو لبْنِة بلدية؟
◇ خِلْصوا العكّاوي اليوْم، بسّ في عِنّا حلوم. بيهِمّك؟
o أيْه پْليز، باخُد بسّ نُصّ كيلو.
◇ بِأمْرِك. شي تاني مدام؟
o لأ مرْسي، قدّيْ كِلُّن سَوى؟
◇ خمْسْتعْشر ألْف، بسّ مِش هوْن بْتِدْفعي. أنا بْسعِّرْلِك، وبْتِدْفعي عالصّنْدوق.
o اه مظْبوط. مرْسي كْتير.
◇ تِكْرم عَيْنِك مدام.

(She looks at the clerk assisting her.)

o أوْكي، آخِر شي فيك تْفرْجيني ويْن قِسْم الخُضْرا والفْواكِه؟
◇ أكيد. لْحقيني[5].

(They walk over to the produce section.)

o مرْحبا مْعلّم، فيك تْساعِدْني نقّي خُضْرا وبقْلِة؟
◇ أكيد، شو بْتِحِبّي أعْطيكي؟
o فِي پْليز آخُد ضُمّْتيْن بقْدونِس وضُمِّةْ نعْنع. وكمان باخُد كيلو تِفّاح وكيلو نْجاص. وإذا عِنْدك بطّيخ مْنيح، باخُد راس[6] عَ ذَوْقك.
◇ تِكْرم عَيْنِك.

o Good morning! I have never been to this supermarket, and I need some help, please.
◇ Good morning, miss! No worries at all. I can help you out. What can I do for you?
o I first want to know where the meat and cheese sections are?
◇ Right over here. Let's walk together.

(They walk over to the meat department.)

- o Good morning, sir. Can I please have one kilo of barbecue beef?
- ◇ Anything else?
- o Yeah. I'd like two kilos of sausages.
- ◇ You're in luck. We got great sausages in this morning.
- o Awesome. How much do I owe you?
- ◇ I'll price it here, and you can pay at the cashier when you're done with all your shopping.
- o Great! Thank you.

(She looks at the clerk assisting her.)

- o Okay. I think I'll get cheese later. I'll do the necessities now. Where can I find labneh?
- ◇ Well, you have two options: you can either get it from the cheese section, where they package it for you on the spot, and that's usually the fresher kind. Or, you can get it pre-packaged from the refrigerator over there.
- o Okay, let's go to the cheese section then. And I'll get the cheese and labneh all at once.

(They walk over to the cheese section.)

- ◇ Hi, ma'am. What can I get for you?
- o Can I please have 1 kg of Akkawi cheese and 2 kg organic, local Labne?
- ◇ We're all out of Akkawi for the day. But we have Halloumi. Are you interested?
- o Yes, please. I'll only take half a kilo, though.
- ◇ My pleasure. Anything else, ma'am?
- o No, thank you. How much is total then?
- ◇ It's 15,000 L.L., but you don't need to pay here. I'll price here, and you can just pay at the cashier.
- o Oh, that's right. Thank you very much.
- ◇ My pleasure, ma'am.

(She looks at the clerk assisting her.)

- o Okay, and finally, can you please show me the produce section?

◇ Certainly! Follow me.

(They walk over to the produce section.)

○ Hello, sir. Can you please help me pick out some vegetables and herbs?

◇ Of course! What can I get for you?

○ Can I please have two bunches of parsley and one bunch of mint? I'll also take one kg of apples and one kg of pears. And, if you have good watermelon, I'd like a nice watermelon.

◇ You got it.

○ *ṣabāḫu! wála márra jīt 3a háydi -s[supermarket] ʔábil*[1]*, w báddi šwáyyit msē3adi.*

◇ *ṣabāḫu, [ᶠdemoiselle]. wála yhímmik ábadan. ána bsē3dik*[2]*. kīf fíyi sē3dik?*

○ *áwwal šī báddi á3rif wēn ʔism illáḫmi w iljíbni.*

◇ *hōn, xallīna nímši sáwa.*

(They walk over to the meat department.)

○ *[ᶠbonjour] m3állim, [please] fíyi ēxud kīlu láḫmi báʔar la-ššáwi?*

◇ *šī tēni?*

○ *ē, báddi tnēn kīlu maʔēni?.*

◇ *ḫáẓẓik ḫílu, ijēna maʔēni? ɣēr šíkl*[3] *ilyōm iṣṣúbuḫ.*

○ *tamēm, ʔaddē báddak mínni?*

◇ *bsa33írlik yēhun hōn, bass fīki tídfa3i 3a-ṣṣandūʔ bass txállṣi kill ɣrāḍik.*

○ *tamēm, [ᶠmerci].*

(She looks at the clerk assisting her.)

○ *okē, bíftikir raḫ jīb iljíbni ba3dēn. raḫ jīb ilʔíšya -ḍḍarūríyyi hálla?. wēn fíyi lēʔi lábni.*

◇ *3índik iḫtimēlēn: ímma btēxdiya min ʔism iljíbni, fúliṭ*[4] *w biwaḍḍbūlik yēha hunīk díɣri. háwdi ijmēlan bikūnu ṭāza áktar, aw fīki tēxdi yálli mwaḍḍabīn bi-lbirrād hunīk.*

○ *okē, xallīna nrūḫ 3a barrād iljíbni fa-ízan, w hēk bjīb jíbni w lábni fard márra.*

(They walk over to the cheese section.)

◇ *áhla, [ᶠmadame], šū fíyi a3ṭīki?*

○ *fíyi [please] ēxud kīlu 3akkēwi w tnēn kīlu lábni baladíyyi?*

◇ *xílṣu -l3akkēwi -lyōm, bass fī 3ínna ḫalūm. bihímmik?*

○ *ē, [please], bēxud bass nuṣṣ kīlu.*
◇ *bi-ámrik. šī tēni, [ᶠmadame]?*
○ *laʔ [ᶠmerci], ʔaddē kíllun sáwa?*
◇ *xámsta3šar alf, bass miš hōn btídfa3i. ána bsá33irlik, w btídfa3i 3a-ṣṣandūʔ.*
○ *āh maẓbūṭ. [ᶠmerci] ktīr.*
◇ *tíkram 3áynik, [ᶠmadame].*

(She looks at the clerk assisting her.)

◇ *okē, ēxir šī fīk tfarjīni wēn ʔism ilxúḍra w lifwēki?*
○ *akīd. lḫaʔīni*[5].

(They walk over to the produce section.)

◇ *márḫaba m3állim, fīk tsē3idni náʔʔi xúḍra w báʔli?*
○ *akīd, šū bitḫíbbi a3ṭīki?*
◇ *fíyi [please] ēxud ḍummtēn baʔdūnis w ḍúmmit ná3na3. w kamēn bēxud kīlu tiffēḫ w kīlu njāṣ. w íza 3índak baṭṭīx mnīḫ, bēxud rāṣ*[6] *3a záwʔak.*
○ *tíkram 3áynik.*

[1] هَيْدي أوّل مرّة بِجي لهوْن. *háydi áwwal márra bíji la-hōn.* **This is the first time I've come here.**

[2] = إخدِمِك *ixídmik*

[3] غيرْ شِكِل *ɣēr šíkil* **great, amazing**. Notice that شكِل *šákil* **shape, appearance** is normally pronounced with fatha (*a*) in the first syllable, but with kasra (*i*) in this expression.

[4] فلِت *fálit* **not pre-packaged**

[5] = تعي معي *tá3i má3i*

[6] راس *rās* **head** is the counter word for watermelons (just as in English, we say a head of lettuce, for example).

Vocabulary

supermarket	*[supermarket]*	سوپِرْمارْكِت
shopping cart	*karrāji* *3arabēyi*	كرّاجِة عربايِة
checkout stand	*ṣandū? (ṣnēdī?)* *[cashier]*	صَنْدوق (صْناديق) كاشير
change (money back)	*-lbē?i*	الباقي
small bills, coins	*frāṭa*	فْراطة
kilo(gram)	*kīlu*	كيلو
to weigh	*zēn (yzīn)*	زان (يْزين)
produce section (of a supermarket)	*?ísm ilxúḍra*	قِسْم الخُضْرة
greengrocer, vegetable seller	*xúḍarji*	خُضَرْجي
vegetables	*xúḍra*	خُضْرة
fruit(s)	*fwēki*	فْواكِه
to select, pick	*ná??a (yná??i)*	نقّى (يْنقّي)
to peel	*?áššar (y?áššir)*	قشّر (يْقشِّر)
fresh	*ṭāza*	طازة
wilted, dry	*dablēn*	دبْلان
organic	*[ᶠorganique]* *báladi*	أوْرْجانيك بلدي
season	*máwsam (mawēsim)*	مَوْسم (مَواسِم)

cheese	*jíbni (ajbēn)*	جِبْنِة (أجْبان)
yogurt	*lában (albēn)*	لبن (ألْبان)
tub, container	*sáţil (sţūl)*	سطِل (سْطول)
sweets	*ђílu (ђilwayēt)*	حِلو (حِلْوَيات)
chewing gum	*3ílki (3ílak)*	عِلْكِة (علِك)
toy	*lí3bi (al3āb)*	لِعْبِة (ألْعاب)

Expressions

Could you weigh one kilo of __ for me?	*fīk tzínli kīlu__?*	فيك تْزِنْلي كيلو__؟
Can I have a kilo of Labne and a kilo of Halloumi?	*fíyi ēxud kīlu lábni w kīlu ђallūmi?*	فِيي آخُد كيلو لبْنِة وكيلو حلّومي؟
Where is the toys aisle?	*wēn maђţūţīn illí3ab/ilʔal3āb?*	ويْن محْطوطين اللِّعب/الألْعاب؟
Do you guys sell Alfa recharge cards?	*bitbī3u xţūţ tišrīj [Alfa]?*	بِتْبيعوا خْطوط تِشْريج ألْفا؟
Do you guys have Western Union here?	*3índkun [Western Union] hōn?*	عِنْدْكُن ويْسْترْن يونْيون هوْن؟
Where can I find spices?	*wēn fíyi lēʔi libhārāt?*	ويْن فِيي لاقي البْهارات؟
May I pay with dollars?	*fíyi ídfa3 bi-ddólar?*	فِيي إدْفع بِالدّوْلار؟
Do you take checks?	*btēxdu [^F chèque]ēt?*	بْتاخْدوا شاكات؟

At the Butcher's عِنْد اللّحّام

لحّامين *laħħāmīn* **butchers** in Lebanon are either located in standalone butcheries, or inside supermarkets and minimarkets. Butchers take a lot of pride in the quality of their لحْمِة *láħmi* **meat**, that it is طازة *ṭāza* ***fresh*** or شِغْل اليوْم *šiɣl ilyōm* **butchered today**, and may boast that it is مِن الضَّيْعة *min iḍḍáy3a* **from the countryside**. Sometimes, they will even tell you بعْدْنا دابْحين *bá3dna dēbħīn* **just slaughtered**. While Lebanon has a large Muslim population (a little over half of the population), butchers still serve لحِم خنْزير *láħim xanzīr* **pork**, especially in towns that are predominantly Christian. If you're looking for halal or non-pork meat, make sure you specify that to your butcher. The Lebanese get quite creative with beef, lamb, and chicken: كفْتة *káfta* **kofta** (beef or lamb meatballs with parsley, onions, and spices); كبِّة *kábbi* (spiced ground beef covered with cracked wheat); مقانق *maʔēniʔ* and سِجِقّ *sijíʔʔ* (kinds of Lebanese sausages; and everyone's favorites: مشاوي *mašēwi* (barbecued meat on skewers, or what we call in English kebabs). But be mindful: If you say كباب *kabēb,* in Lebanon, this is a specific type of meat on skewers: ground spiced chicken.

Buying meat

- ○ بْقدّيْ كيلو اللّحْمِة المفْرومِة إذا بِتْرِيد[1]؟
- ◇ سبعْتلاف وخمْسْمية.
- ○ أوْكيْ، پْليز زِنْلي نُصّ كيلو مْن اللّحْمِة الحمْرا مِن هونيك، وفْرِمْلي ياها پْليز.
- ◇ تحِت أمْرِك.[2]

- ○ How much is one kilo of ground meat?
- ◇ 7,500 L.L.
- ○ Okay, weigh half a kilo from the red meat over there and grind it for me, please.
- ◇ My pleasure!

- ○ *b-ʔaddē kīlu -lláɧmi -lmafrūmi íza bi-trīd[1]?*
- ◇ *saba3talēf w xamsmíyyi.*
- ○ *okē, [please] zínli nuṣṣ kīlu mn illáɧmi -lɧámra min hunīk, w frímli yēha, [please].*
- ◇ *táɧit ámrik.[2]*

[1] = عْموْل معْروف *3mōl ma3rūf*

[2] = تِكْرمي *tíkrami*

2

Having a sheep slaughtered

- ○ كان بدّي شوف كيف السّيسْتِم[1] إذا بدّي إدْبح خروف.
- ◇ بْتِجي بِتْشوف وبِتْنقّي واحد، مْنِدْبحْلك ياه، مْنِسْلخو، مْنرْجع مِنْقطّعو ومِنْقسّمو وكِلّ شي.
- ○ أوْكي، الِمْهِمّ إنّو بسّ آخِدُن ما يْكون بدّي أعْمِل شي.[2]
- ◇ هَيْدا اللي رح يْصير! بْتاخِدُن مِن هوْن كمان مْوَضّبين[3] ومحْطوطين بِصَواني للْكبّ وسالوفان. فما بْتِعْطل همّ شي إلّا إنّو تِشْوي وتاكُل.

- ○ I wanted to know how it works if I want to have a sheep slaughtered.
- ◇ You come see and choose one, and then we slaughter it for you, skin, butcher, and divide it up–everything.
- ○ Okay, as long as when I take it, I won't have to do anything!
- ◇ That's exactly what's going to happen! And, you'll receive them packaged on disposable trays covered with plastic wrap. You won't have to worry about doing anything, except grilling and eating.

- ○ *kēn báddi šūf kīf is[system][1] íza báddi ídbaḫ xarūf.*
- ◇ *btíji bitšūf w bitnáʔʔi wāḫad, mnidbáḫlak yēh, mníslaxu, mnírja3 minʔáṭṭ3u w minʔássmu w kill šī.*
- ○ *okē, limhímm ínnu bass ēxidun ma ykūn báddi á3mil šī.*[2]
- ◇ *háyda -lli raḫ yṣīr! btēxidun min hōn kamēn mwaḍḍabīn*[3] *w maḫṭūṭīn bi-ṣawēni la-lkább w [Fcellophane]. fa-má btí3ṭal hamm šī ílla ínnu tíšwi w tēkul.*

[1] = شو الطّريقة *šū -ṭṭarīʔa*

[2] الِمْهِمّ يْكون جاهِز وما يِحْتاج شي. *limhímm ykūn jēhiz w ma yiḫtēj šī.*

[3] = مضْبوبين *maḍbūbīn*

3

Buying chicken

○ بدّي تْلاتِة كيلو دْجاج، فْخاد پْليز.

◇ عِنّا عرِض عالفرّوج الكامِل اليوْم.

○ لأ ما مِنْحِبّ الصِّدِر. بسّ الِفْخاد پْليز.[1]

◇ أوْكيْ، بِتْحِبّي شي تاني؟[2]

○ لأ مرْسي، بسّ خلِّصْن بْسِرْعة پْليز لِأنّو جايِة لعِنْدي ناس[3] اللَّيْلِة.

○ I want 3 kilos of chicken, thighs, please.

◇ There is a special on whole chickens today.

○ No, we don't like breasts. Just the thighs, please.

◇ Okay, anything else?

○ No, thanks. Just please get them ready quickly, as I have people coming over this evening.

○ *báddi tlēti kīlu djēj, fxād, [please].*

◇ *3ínna 3áriḍ 3a-lfarrūj ilkēmil ilyōm.*

○ *laʔ ma minɧíbb íṣṣidir. bass lifxād, [please].*[1]

◇ *okē, bitɧíbbi šī tēni?*[2]

○ *laʔ [Fmerci], bass xálliṣun b-sír3a [please] li-ánnu jēyi la-3índi nēs*[3] *illáyli.*

[1] شو العرِض؟ انْشالله يْكون مِحْرِز! *šū -l3áriḍ? nšálla ykūn míɧriz!* **What's the offer? I hope it's a good deal!**

[2] = بْتِئِمْرينا بْشي تاني؟ *btiʔmrīna b-šī tēni?*

[3] = عِنْدي معازيم *3índi ma3azīm* **I have guests/company**

4

Choosing animals to slaughter

o بدّي حبْشِة عَ ذَوْقك پْليز.

◇ يَحِنّ[1] هوْن، نقّي واحد.

o أوْكي، پْليز وزِنْلي هَيْدا وسعِّرْلي ياه، وبدّي كمان صِدْريْن[2]

o I'd like a nice turkey, please.

◇ Here they are. Choose one.

o Okay, weigh this one and price it for me, please. I'll also add a couple of chicken breasts.

o *báddi ħábši 3a záwʔak, [please].*

◇ *yaħínni[1] hōn, náʔʔi wāħad.*

o *okē, [please] w zínli háyda w sa33írli yēh, w báddi kamēn ṣidrēn[2].*

[1] يَحِنّ! *yaħínni!* **here they are!**; يَحْوّ! *yaħúwwi!* **here he/it is!**; يَحِيّ! *yaħíyyi!* **here she/it is!**

[2] = سْفينْتيْن *sfīntēn*

5

Having meat cut to specification

o پْليز قطِّعْلي هَيْدي تِقْطيع رَفيع.
◇ أوْكيْ، بدِّك كمان شيل الدِّهِن؟
o لأ خلِّيْنْ للشّوي، بسّ قسِّمْلي ياهُن عَ صحْنينْ[1]، لَوْ سمحِت.

o Please, slice these into really thin slices.
◇ Okay, you want me to remove the fat?
o No, leave it on for grilling, but split them onto two plates, please.

o *[please] ʔaṭṭí3li háydi tiʔṭī3 rafī3.*
◇ *okē, báddik kamēn šīl iddíhin?*
o *laʔ xallíyun la-ššáwi, bass ʔassímli yēhun 3a ṣaḫnēn[1], law samáḫit.*

[1] = حُطّ كِلّ واحد لحال *ḫuṭṭ kill wāḫad la-ḫāl* **separate them** (lit. put each one on its own)

6

BUYING VARIOUS MEAT PRODUCTS

- o بدّي تْنينْ كيلو كفْتة ونُصّ كيلو سَوْدا.
- ◇ سوْري بسّ ما عِنّا سَوْدا بقى.
- o طيِّب معْليْه، بسّ كفْتة فإذاً. ونُصّ كيلو لحْمِة بقر مفْروم.
- ◇ عِنّا كمان مقانِق إجوا هلّق مِن ساعة. بيجِنّنوا[1].
- o أوْكي، باخُد[2] نُصّ كيلو مقانِق فإذاً.

- o I want two kilos of kofta and half a kilo of liver.
- ◇ I'm sorry, but there isn't any liver left.
- o It's okay. Just the kofta, then, and half a kilo of ground beef.
- ◇ We have sausages that came in just an hour ago. They look great.
- o Okay, I'll take half a kilo of sausages, then.

- o *báddi tnēn kīlu káfta w nuṣṣ kīlu sáwda.*
- ◇ *[sorry] bass ma 3ínna sáwda báʔa.*
- o *ṭáyyib ma3lē, bass káfta fa-ízan. w nuṣṣ kīlu láḥmi báʔar mafrūm.*
- ◇ *3ínna kamēn maʔēniʔ íju hállaʔ min sē3a. bijánninu*[1].
- o *okē, bēxud*[2] *nuṣṣ kīlu maʔēniʔ fa-ízan.*

[1] = بْيِعجْبوا خاطْرِك *byí3ijbu xāṭrik* **you'll love them**

[2] عْطيني *3ṭīni* **give me...**

- o لَوْ سمحِت، بدّي طاووق. بْقدّيْ الكيلو؟
- ◇ بدِّك ياهُن مْتبّلين أَوْ عادي؟
- o واوْ! عِنْدك مْتبّل؟ بْقدّيْ الكيلو؟
- ◇ اللي مْتبّل بِسوْس[1] حمْرا، عشِرْتلاف ليرة، واللي مْتبّل بِلبن، تسِعْتلاف.
- o أوْكيْ، باخُد نُصّ كيلو مِن كلِّ واحد.
- ◇ تِكْرم عَيْنِك. بِتْحِبّي شي تاني؟
- o أيْه بدّي كفْتة كمان پْليز، بسّ بسّ إذا طازة.
- ◇ دابْحينُن اليوْم، كلّو طازة.
- o أوْكيْ، هات تَشوف شو بدّي بعْد. بدّي كيلو لحْمِة مفْرومِة.
- ◇ ما عِنّا لحْمِة مفْرومِة بقى، بسّ إذا بِتْحِبّي، فيكي تْنقّي الشّقْفِة اللي بدِّك ياها، وبِفْرمْلِك ياها.
- o أوْكيْ، باخُد كيلو مْن اللّحْمِة اللي عالصّنية هونيكِة. كيلو واحد وبلا دِهِن.
- ◇ هَيْدي مْنيحة؟[3]
- o عظيم. وآخِر شي بدّي ياه هُوِّ كيلو قصْبِة دْجاج، إذا عِنْدك.
- ◇ بسّ قصْبِة؟ أَوْ قَوانِص كمان؟
- o إذا عِنْدك قَوانِص طازة، باخُد نُصّ كيلو.
- ◇ أيْه شِغْل اليوْم.
- o يِسْلمو إيديْك، وعِنْدك إسْكالوپ شي؟
- ◇ أيْه في. قدّيْ بدِّك زين؟[4]
- o نُصّ كيلو. وقطّعو رفيع عْموْل معْروف.
- ◇ تِكْرم عَيْنِك. رح دِقِّلِك ياه كمان، هيْك بيكون جاهِز للتّتْبيل.

o أوْكي، مرْسي كْتير. قدّيْ بْيِطْلعوا كِلْن سَوى؟[5]

◇ كِلّو مْسعّر، بسّ المجْموع بْتاخْديه عالصّنْدوق. إذا في شي ما بدِّك ياه، فيكي تِترْكيه ساعِتا، ما في مشْكل.

o أوْكي، مرْسي كْتير.

o Excuse me. I'd like some chicken tawouk. How much is a kilo?

◇ Seasoned or regular?

o Wow, you have seasoned? How much are those?

◇ Seasoned with red sauce is 10,000 L.L. per kilo, and seasoned with yogurt sauce is 9,000 L.L.

o Okay, I'll take half a kilo of each.

◇ My pleasure. Anything else?

o Yes, I want some kofta, as well, but only if they're fresh, please.

◇ They were slaughtered today! All fresh!

o Okay, let's see what else I want... I also want one kilo of ground meat.

◇ There isn't any ground meat at the moment, but if you'd like, you can choose any cut, and I can grind it up for you.

o Okay, I'll have some of the meat on that tray over there. One kilo but without any fat.

◇ Is this good?

o Perfect. And the last thing I want is one kilo of chicken livers, if there are any.

◇ Just livers? Or giblets, too?

o If you have fresh giblets, I'll take just half a kilo.

◇ Yes, today's slaughter.

o Bless your hands. And also, if there are any escalopes?

◇ Yes, there are. How much shall I weigh?

o Half a kilo, and slice it thin, please.

◇ My pleasure. I'll pound it for you, too, so that it is ready to be seasoned.

○ Okay, thanks so much. How much does that come out to now?

◇ Everything is labeled with a price, but the total you'll get at the cashier. If you want to leave anything behind at that time, it's no problem.

○ Okay, thanks a lot.

○ *law samáħit, báddi ţawū?. b-?addē -lkīlu?*

◇ *báddik yēhun mtabbalīn aw 3ādi?*

○ *wāw! 3índak mtábbal? b-?addē -lkīlu?*

◇ *ílli mtábbal bi-şōş*[1] *ħámra, 3aširtalēf līra, w -lli mtábbal bi-lában, tisi3talēf.*

○ *okē, bēxud nuşş kīlu min kill wāħad.*

◇ *tíkram 3áynik. bitħíbbi šī tēni?*

○ *ē, báddi káfta kamēn [please], bass báss*[2] *íza ţāza.*

◇ *dēbħīnun ilyōm, kíllu ţāza.*

○ *okē, hēt ta-šūf šū báddi ba3d. báddi kīlu láħmi mafrūmi.*

◇ *ma 3ínna láħmi mafrūmi bá?a, bass íza bitħíbbi, fīki tná??i -ššá?fi -lli báddik yēha, w bifrímlik yēha.*

○ *okē, bēxud kīlu mn illáħmi -lli 3a-şşaníyyi hunīki. kīlu wāħad w bála díhin.*

◇ *háydi mnīħa?*[3]

○ *3azīm. w ēxir šī báddi yēh húwwi kīlu ?áşbit djēj, íza 3índak.*

◇ *bass ?áşbi? aw ?awāniş kamēn?*

○ *íza 3índak ?awāniş ţāza, bēxud nuşş kīlu.*

◇ *ē, šíyl ilyōm.*

○ *yíslamu idēk, w 3índak [*[F]*escalopes] šī?*

◇ *ē, fī. ?addē báddik zīn?*[4]

○ *nuşş kīlu. w ?áţţ3u rafī3, 3mōl ma3rūf.*

◇ *tíkram 3áynik. raħ di??ílik yēh kamēn, hēk bikūn jēhiz la-ttitbīl.*

○ *okē, [*[F]*merci] ktīr. ?addē byíţla3u kíllun sáwa?*[5]

◇ *kíllu msá33ar, bass ilmajmū3 btēxdī 3a-şşandū?. íza fī šī ma báddik yēh, fīki titrkī sē3íta, ma fī máškal.*

○ *okē, [*[F]*merci] ktīr.*

[1] = صلْصة *şálşa*

2 بسّ bass has two meanings, both of which we see here, as the conjunction but and the adverb only. Notice the emphasis on the second word in the audio.

3 شو رأْيك بِهيْدي؟ *šū ráʔyik bi-háydi?* **What do you think of this?** (i.e. How's this?)

4 = كم كيلو بِترْيدي؟ *kam kīlu bitrīdi?*

5 = قدّيْ لِحْساب؟ *ʔaddē liɦsēb?* **How much is the bill?**

Vocabulary

butcher (of red meat)	*laɦɦām*	لحّام
butcher shop	*málɦami*	ملْحمِة
poultry shop	*maɦáll frērīj*	محلّ فْراريج
meat	*láɦim* *láɦmi*	لحِم لحْمِة
beef	*láɦim báʔar*	لحِم بقر
tenderloin	*[tenderloin]*	تِنْدرْلوْيْن
steak	*biftēk*	بِفتيْك
ground meat	*láɦmi mafrūmi* *láɦmi nē3mi*	لحْمِة مفْرومِة لحْمِة ناعْمِة
shank, shin	*mawzēt*	مَوْزات
ribeye, sirloin	*[Fentrecôte]*	أنْترْوكوْت
intestines (stuffed with spiced rice)	*fawēriɣ* *maṣārīn*	فَوارِغ مصارين
lamb	*láɦim ɣánam*	لحِم غنم

sheep	*xarūf*	خروف
chicken	*farrūj* *djēj*	فرّوج دْجاج
a local/organic chicken	*farrūj báladi*	فرّوج بلدي
whole chicken	*farrūj kēmil*	فرّوج كامِل
chicken leg (thigh/drumstick)	*fáxid (fxād)*	فخِد (فْخاد)
(chicken) giblets	*ʔawāniṣ*	قَوانِص
breast	*ṣídir (ṣdūr, ṣdūra)* *sfīni (safēyin)*	صِدِر (صْدور، صْدورة) سْفينِة (سفايِن)
neck	*ráʔbi (rʔēb)*	رقْبِة (رْقاب)
wing	*jnēɧ (ájniɧa)*	جْناح (أجْنِحة)
turkey	*ɧábši* *dīk rūmi (dyūk rūmíyyi)*	حبْشِة ديك رومي (دْيوك رومية)
turkey fillet	*fīlē dīk rūmi*	فيليْه ديك رومي
pigeons	*ɧamēm*	حمام
duck	*baṭṭ*	بطّ
local duck	*baṭṭ báladi*	بطّ بلدي
rabbit	*árnab (arēnib)*	أرْنب (أرانِب)
shish tawouk	*šīš ṭāwūʔ*	شيش طاووق
marrow	*kawēri3*	كَوارِع
brain	*dmēɣ (ádmiɣa)*	دْماغ
lungs	*fíšši*	فِشّة

liver	*kíbid, ʔáṣbi*	كِبِد، قصْبِة
kidneys	*kalēwi*	كلاوي
kebab	*kíbbi*	كباب
meatballs	*káfta*	كفْتة
spiced	*mtábbal*	مْتبّل
frozen	*bi-l[freezer]* *mfárraz*	بِالفْريزر مْفرّز
locally slaughtered	*báladi* *šíɣil hōn* *mn iḍḍáy3a*	بلدي شِغِل هوْن مْن الضّيْعة
to slaughter	*dábaɦ (yídbaɦ)*	دبح (يِدْبح)
slaughtered animal	*dbīɦa (dabēyiɦ)*	دْبيحة (دبايِح)
to grind up, mince	*fáram (yífrum)*	فرم (يِفْرُم)
to skin, flay	*sálax (yíslax)*	سلخ (يِسْلخ)

Expressions

I want two kilos of intestines, and clean them for me, please.	*báddi tnēn kīlu fwēriɣ, w naḍḍífli yēhun, [please].*	بدّي تْنيْن كيلو فَوارِغ، ونضِّفْلي ياهُن، پْليز.
I want two of those turkeys.	*báddi tnēn min háwdi -ddyūk irrūmíyyi, [please].*	بدّي تْنيْن مِن هَوْدي الدُّيوك الرّومية، پْليز.
I'd like the tripe I pre-ordered yesterday.	*báddi -lkiršēyi -lli ṭalábta mbēriɦ.*	بدّي الكِرشايِة اللي طلبتِا مْبارِح.

Excuse me, I ordered chicken liver and giblets, and I've been waiting for nearly half an hour.	*law samáɦit, ţalábit ʔáşbi w ʔawāniş, w şárli taʔrīban nuşş sēʒa nāţir.*	لَوْ سمحِت، طلبِت قصْبِة وقَوانِص، وصرْلي تقْريباً نُصّ ساعة ناطِر .
Give me two kilos of tawouk, one marinated with white sauce and one with hot sauce.	*báddi tnēn kīlu ţāwūʔ, wāɦad bi-sōs báyḑa, w wāɦad bi-sōs ɦárra.*	بدّي تْنينْ كيلو طاووق، واحد بِسوْس بَيْضة، وواحد بِسوْس حرّة.
I want three kilos of sausages.	*báddi tlēti kīlu mʔēniʔ w sijíʔʔ.*	بدّي تْلاتِة كيلو مْقانِق وسِجِقّ.
Is this meat freshly butchered?	*háydi -lláɦmi madbūɦa ţāza?*	هَيْدي اللحْمِة مدْبوحة طازة؟
Is this frozen meat?	*háydi -lláɦmi mjámmadi?*	هَيْدي اللحْمِة مْجمّدِة؟

◇

This duck weighs two kilos.	*háydi -lbáţţa wázna tnēn kīlu.*	هَيْدي البطّة وَزْنا تْنينْ كيلو.

In a Clothing Shop   بِمحلّ تْياب

Retail therapy! A great way to escape from the noise and bustle outside is to duck into a nice محلّ *maħáll* **shop** or spend hours strolling around a large, air-conditioned موْل *mōl* **shopping mall**. Most shops now take debit and credit cards, but it's always a good idea to ask بْتاخْدي كارْت؟ *btēxdi [ᶠcarte]?* **Do you take credit cards?** first–before you get your heart set on that outfit! And just a heads-up: When you enter a محلّ *maħáll* **shop**, a salesperson will likely start to follow you around. This may make you feel a bit uneasy if you're not used to this, but they're not suspicious that you're going to shoplift. It's their job to be available to assist you and answer questions. If you'd like them to back off a bit, just tell them nicely مرْسي عم بِتْفرّج *[ᶠmerci], 3am bitfárraj* **Thank you, I'm just browsing**.

Getting help from a sales clerk

◇ عم بِتْنبّْشي عَ شي مْعيّن؟
○ أيْه، بدّي تنّورة جينْز لوْن غامِق پْليز.
◇ هلّق إجِتْنا تشْكيلِة جْديدِة![1]

◇ Are you looking for something in particular?
○ Yes, please. I'm looking for a dark jean skirt.
◇ We just got our new collection!

◇ *3am bitnábbši 3a šī m3áyyan?*
○ *ē, báddi tannūra jīnz lōn ɣēmi?, [please].*
◇ *hálla? ijítna taškīli jdīdi!*[1]

[1] = هلّق إجِتْنا كوْليْكْسْيوْن جْديدِة! *hálla? ijítna! [Fcollection] jdīdi!*

2

Browsing

◇ عم بِتْفتِّش عَ شي مْحدّد؟
○ لأ، مرْسي. عم بِتْفرّج[1]، وإذا حبّيْت شي بِسْألِك.[2]
◇ أكيد، خوْد وَقْتك مونْسْيور.
○ مرْسي![3]

◇ Is there anything in particular that you're looking for?
○ No, I'm just looking around. If there's something I like, I'll ask you about it.
◇ Sure, take your time, sir.
○ Thank you!

◇ *3am bitfáttiš 3a šī mɦáddad?*
○ *laʔ, [ᶠmerci]. 3am bitfárraj*[1]*, w íza ɦabbēt šī bísʔalik.*[2]
◇ *akīd, xōd wáʔtak, [ᶠmonsieur].*
○ *[ᶠmerci]!*[3]

[1] = عم بِتْفتّل *3am bitfáttal*

[2] أيْ مُمْكِن تْساعْديني؟ *ē, múmkin tsē3dīni?* **Yes, can you help me?**

[3] = شُكْراً *šúkran*

③

Asking about a sale

○ هَوْدي كمان عْلينّ صوْلْد؟
◇ لأ، هوْل مِش داخْلين بِالصّوْلْد.[1]
○ويْن الإشْيا اللي عْلَيا صوْلْد فإذاً.
◇ كِلّ هَيْدي الجِهة عْلَيا صوْلْد لأِنّو عم نْصفِّيْن.

○ Are these on sale?
◇ No, they're not included in the sale.
○ Where are the things on sale then?
◇ This whole side is on sale because they're on clearance.

○ *háwdi kamēn 3láyyun [Fsolde]?*
◇ *laʔ, hōl miš dēxlīn bi-ṣ[Fsolde].[1]*
○ *wēn ilʔíšya -lli 3láya [Fsolde] fa-ízan.*
◇ *kill háydi -ljíha 3láya [Fsolde] li-ánnu 3am nṣaffíyun.*

[1] كِلّ الكوْليْكْسْيوْن القديمِة عْلَيا خصِم. *kill il[Fcollection] ilʔadīmi 3láya xáṣim.*

Asking about sizes

○ هَيْدي بْيِجي مِنّا أكْبر شي؟[1]
◇ في مِنّا لارْج وإكْسْترا لارْج.[2]
○ في مِنّا ميدْيوم شي؟
◇ لأ والله ما في. خالْصين الميدْيوم.[3]

○ Does this come in a larger size?
◇ There is large and XL.
○ There's no medium available?
◇ No, unfortunately, there isn't. We're all out.

○ *háydi byíji mínna ákbar šī?*[1]
◇ *fī mínna lārj w [extra] lārj.*[2]
○ *fī mínna [medium] šī?*
◇ *laʔ wálla, ma fī. xālṣīn il[medium].*[3]

[1] = في مِنّا قْياس أكْبر؟ *fī mínna ʔyēs ákbar?*

[2] هَيْدي المارْكة أصلاً قْياساتا كْبيرِة. *háydi -lmárka áṣlan ʔyēsēta kbīri.* **This brand's sizes actually run a bit big.**

[3] خلّيني شِفْلِك بِغيرْ فِرِع إذا بيهِمّك. *xallīni šíflik bi-ɣēr fíri3 íza bihímmik.* **Let me check at another store of ours, if you're interested.**

5

Buying shoes

○ عِنْدك شي مِن هَيْدا بسّ جِلِد لمّيع؟

◇ لأ، عِنّا لمّيع، بسّ كعِب عالي.[1]

○ لأ حابِّة زحِف.

◇ لازِم يْكون جِلِد لمّيع؟ لِأنّو عِنّا مِنّو دان كْتير شيك.

○ عن جدّ حِلْوين. عِنْدك مِنُّن قْياس تْمانة وتْلاتين؟

○ Do you have one like these but in patent leather?

◇ No, there are patent leather ones but with high heels.

○ No, I'm looking for flats.

◇ Do they have to be patent leather? We have them in suede, and they look so stylish.

○ They do look nice. Do you have them in size 38?

○ *3índak šī min háyda bass jílid lammī3?*

◇ *laʔ, 3ínna lammī3, bass ká3ib 3āli.*[1]

○ *laʔ ɦābbi záɦif.*

◇ *lēzim ykūn jílid lammī3? li-ánnu 3ínna mínnu [Fdaim] ktīr [Fchic].*

○ *3an jadd ɦilwīn. 3índak mínnun ʔyēs tmēna w tlētīn?*

[1] أيْه عِنّا! يَلّا هلّق بْجِبْلِك قْياسِك. *ē, 3ínna! yálla hállaʔ bjíblik ʔyēsik.* **Yes, we do! I'll get your size for you.**

6

Asking about materials

o هَيْدا جِلِد أَصْلي؟

◇ نعم إسْتاذ.

o وَطني أَوْ مُسْتَوْرِد؟[1]

◇ شِغِل لِبْنان إسْتاذ. مْصنّع بِالمعْمل تبعْنا بِالكاسْليك. بسّ إذا حابِب شي مُسْتَوْرِد، في عِنّا كذا شغْلِة بِالرّايوْن التّاني.

o لأ حبّيْت هَيْدا ورح آخْدو. بدّي قْشاط كمان بِنفْس اللّوْن پْليز.[2]

o Are these genuine leather?

◇ Yes, sir.

o Local or imported?

◇ Lebanese, sir, produced in our factory in Kaslik. But if you want imported leather, we have some options in the next aisle.

o No, I like these; I'll take them, and I also want a belt with the same tone.

o *háyda jílid áşli?*

◇ *ná3am istēz.*

o *wáţani aw mustáwrad?*[1]

◇ *šíɣil libnēn istēz. mşánna3 bi-lmá3mal tabá3na bi-lkēslīk. bass íza ɦābib šī mustáwrad, fī 3ínna káza šáɣli bi-r[^F rayon] ittēni.*

o *laʔ, ɦabbēt háyda w raɦ ēxdu. báddi ʔšāţ kamēn bi-náfs illōn, [please].*[2]

[1] = شِغِل لِبْنان أَوْ مِن برّا؟ *šíɣil libnēn aw min bárra?*

[2] = لأ حبّيْت هَيْدا ورح آخِدو. بدّي سيْنْتور كمان بِذات اللّوْن پْليز. *laʔ, ɦabbēt háyda w raɦ ēxidu. báddi [^F ceinture] kamēn bi-zēt illōn, [please].*

◇ عم بِتْنبْشي[1] عَ شي مْعينّ؟

○ لأ مرْسي، عم بِتْفرّج بسّ.

◇ أكيد، تْفضّلي، أهْلا وسهْلا.

○ بلّش السّايْل؟

◇ بلّش، بسّ مِش عَ كِلّ شي.[2]

○ ويْن الإشْيا اللي عْلَيا سايْل؟

◇ كِلّ هَيْدي السّيكْشُن. بْتِشْتْري قْطْعْتيْن، بْيِطْلعْلِك التّالْتِة بِبلاش[3].

○ حِلو! أوْكي، فِي جرِّب هَيْدي البِلْوزِة[4]؟

◇ أكيد دْمْوازيْل. أُوَض[5] القْياس هونيك.

○ أوْكي خلّيني إتْفرّج بعْد شْوَيّ وبْقيس فرْد مرّة.

(comes out of changing room)

◇ ظبطوا؟[6]

○ هَيْدي التّنّورة مِش مْبيْنِة حِلْوِة عْلَيي أبداً.

◇ بِتْحِبّي تْجرْبي قْياس تاني؟[7]

○ لأ مِش حِلْوِة عْلَيي أبداً. ما بِفْتِكِر القْياس رح يِفْرُق. بسّ بْجرِّب غيرْ قْياس مِن هَيْدا القميص إذا عِنْدِك ياه قْياس واحد أزْغر.[8]

◇ أيْه في، تْفضّلي.

(comes out of changing room again)

◇ ساقبِتِك؟

○ أيْه هَيْدا القْياس أحْسن بِكْتير. باخُد هَيْدي البْلوزِة فإذاً بِأسْوَد وأبْيَض وهَيْدي التّيشيرْت.

◇ أكيد دْمْوازيْل. تْفضّلي عالصّنْدوق[10] وأنا بِلْحقِك.

(goes to cashier)

○ بْتاخْدي كارْت[11]؟

◇ سوْري لأ. ما مْناخُد كارْت.

o أوْكيْ، في مجال تِترِكيلي ياهُن شْوَيّ؟ بِسْحب مصاري مِن أي تي أم قريبِة، وبِرْجع بِدْفع وباخِدُن.[12]

◇ عَ مهْلِك دْمْوازيْل.

◇ Are you looking for something in particular?

o No, thanks, I'm just browsing.

◇ Sure, come on in.

o Has the sale started yet?

◇ It has, but it doesn't include everything.

o Where is the stuff on sale then?

◇ All of this section. Buy two, get the third for free.

o Nice! Okay, can I try on this blouse?

◇ Certainly, miss. The fitting rooms are over there.

o All right. I'll look around some more [first], then I'll try everything at once.

(comes out of changing room)

◇ How are they?

o Well, this skirt doesn't look nice on me at all.

◇ Would you like another size?

o No, it doesn't look nice to begin with; I don't think the size will make a difference, but I can try this blouse in another size if you have it one size smaller.

◇ Yes, there is. Here you are.

(comes out of changing room aqain)

◇ Does it fit?

o Yes, this size fits much better. I'll take this blouse then in black and in white, and also this t-shirt.

◇ Sure, miss. You can go to the cashier, and I'll follow you.

(goes to cashier)

o Do you take credit cards?

◇ I'm sorry, no, we don't take credit cards.

○ Okay, is there somewhere you can keep these for me? I'll withdraw some cash from a nearby ATM and come back to pay for them.

◇ No hurry, miss.

◇ *3am bitnábbši*[1] *3a šī m3áyyan?*

○ *laʔ [Fmerci], 3am bitfárraj bass.*

◇ *akīd, tfáḍḍali, áhla w sáhla.*

○ *bállaš is[sale]?*

◇ *bállaš, bass miš 3a kill šī.*[2]

○ *wēn ilʔíšya -lli 3láya [sale]?*

◇ *kill háydi -s[section]. btíštri ʔuṭ3tēn, byíṭla3lik ittēlti bi-balēš*[3].

○ *ɧílu! okē, fíyi járrib háydi -liblūzi*[4]?

◇ *akīd, [Fdemoiselle]. úwaḍ*[5] *liʔyēs hunīk.*

○ *okē xallīni itfárraj ba3d šwayy w bʔīs fard márra.*

(comes out of changing room)

◇ *ẓabáṭu?*[6]

○ *háydi -ttannūra miš mbáyyni ɧílwi 3láyi ábadan.*

◇ *bitɧíbbi tjárrbi ʔyēs tēni?*[7]

○ *laʔ, miš ɧílwi 3láyi ábadan. ma bíftikir liʔyēs raɧ yífruʔ. bass bjárrib ɣēr ʔyēs min háyda -lʔamīṣ íza 3índik yēh ʔyēs wāɧad ázɣar.*[8]

◇ *ē, fī, tfáḍḍali.*

(comes out of changing room again)

◇ *sēʔábitik?*

○ *ē, háyda -liʔyēs áɧsan bi-ktīr. bēxud háydi -lblūzi fa-ízan bi-áswad w ábyaḍ w háydi -t[t-shirt].*

◇ *akīd, [Fdemoiselle]. tfáḍḍali 3a-ṣṣandūʔ*[10] *w ána bílɧaʔik.*

(goes to cashier)

○ *btēxdi [Fcarte]*[11]*?*

◇ *[sorry] laʔ. ma mnēxud [Fcarte].*

○ *okē, fī majēl titirkīli yēhun šwayy? bísɧab maṣāri min [AṭM] ʔarībi, w bírja3 bídfa3 w bēxidun.*[12]

◇ *3a máhlik, [Fdemoiselle].*

[1] = بِتْفتّْشي *bitfáttši*

[2] لأ بعِد. لآخِر الشّهِر. *laʔ, ba3id. la-ēxir iššahir.* **Not yet, not until the end of the month.**

[3] مجّاناً *majjēnan*

4 = هَيْدا القميص *háyda -lʔamīṣ*

5 = غُرَف *ɣúraf*

6 = مِشي حالُن؟ *míši ħālun?* = إجوا عالْقدّ؟ *íju 3a-lʔadd?* = ساقبوكي؟ *sēʔabūki?*

7 بِتْحِبّي تْجرْبي غيرْ قْياس؟ *bitħíbbi tjárrbi ɣēr ʔyēs?*

8 عِنْدِك مِنّا غيرْ ألْوان؟ *3índik mínna ɣēr alwēn?* **Do you have other colors?**

9 = ظبطِت عْلَيْكي؟ *ẓábaṭit 3láyki?*

10 = حاسْبِة *ħāsbi*

11 = بِطاقة *biṭāʔa*

12 = خِدي وَقْتِك *xídi wáʔtik.*; سوْري دْموازيْل. ما فينا نِحْجِز تْياب أبداً. هَيْدي قَوانين المحلّ، وأنا مْوَظّفة هوْن. *[sorry], [ᶠdemoiselle]. ma fīna níħjiz tyēb ábadan. háydi ʔawēnīs ilmaħáll, w ána mwáẓẓfi hōn.* **I'm sorry, miss. We're not allowed to hold any items. This is store policy, and I'm just the employee here.**

Vocabulary

to buy	*štára (yíštri)*	شْترى (يِشْترْي)
to go shopping (lit. to buy things)	*štára (yíštri) ɣrāḑ*	شْترى (يِشْترْي) غْراض
to pay	*dáfa3 (yídfa3)*	دفع (يِدْفع)
cash	*[cash]*	كاش
credit card	*[credit card]*	كْريْدِت كارْد
price	*sí3ir (as3ār)*	سِعِر (أسْعار)
cheap	*rxīş (rxāş)*	رْخيص (رْخاص)
expensive	*ɣāli*	غالي
sale, discount	*xáşim (xşūmēt)* *ɦásim (ɦsūmēt)*	خصِم (خْصومات) حسِم (حْسومات)
store, shop	*maɦáll*	محلّ
customer	*zbūn (zabēyin)*	زْبون (زبايِن)
shirt	*ʔamīş (ʔumşān)* *[Fchemise]*	قميص (قْمْصان) شميز
blouse	*blūz* *blūzi*	بْلوز بْلوزِة
t-shirt	*[t-shirt]*	تيشيرْت
pants	*banţalōn* *[Fpantalon]*	بنْطلوْن پنْطلوْن
jeans	*[jeans]*	جينْز
shorts	*[short]*	شوْرْت

skirt	*tannūra (tnēnīr)*	تنّورة (تنانير)
dress	*fisṭān (fasāṭīn)*	فِسْطان (فساطين)
belt	*ʔšāṭ*	أشاط
sweatshirt	*[sweatshirt]*	سْويتْشيرْت
sweater	*kánzi*	كنْزِة
jacket	*[jacket]*	جاكيْتّ
coat	*montō (montoyēt)*	مانْتوْ (مانْتوْيات)
shoes	*jázmi, [shoes], ṣubbāṭ*	جزْمِة، شوز، صُبّاط
sneakers, tennis shoes	*spádri* *ṣubbāṭ ryāḍa*	سْپَدْرِي صُبّاط رْياضة
boots	*bōt*	بوْت
boots	*bōtīn*	بوْتين
half boots	*[ᶠdemi]bōt*	دومي بوْتين
sandal	*ṣandāl*	صنْدال
ballerina flats	*[ᶠballerines]* *[ballerina]*	بالورين بالورينا
heel	*ká3ib (k3ūb)*	كعِب (كْعوب)
shoelaces	*rábṭit [ᶠbottes]/* *[shoes]/ṣubbāṭ*	ربْطِةْ بوْت/ شوز/صُبّاط
handbag, purse	*jizdēn (jzēdīn)*	جِزْدان (جْزادين)
wallet	*míḫfaẓa*	مِحْفظة
scarf	*šēl*	شيْل

headscarf	*ɧjēb*	حْجاب
(natural) leather	*jild (ţabī3i)*	جِلْد (طبيعي)
suede	*[Fchamois]*	شمْواه
glossy leather	*jild lammī3*	جِلْد لمّيع
cotton	*ʔúţun*	قُطْن
linen	*kittēn*	كِتّان
chiffon	*[Fchiffon]*	شيفوْن
perfume	*[Fparfum]*	پرْفان
(pair of) glasses	*3waynēt [3waynētēt]*	عْوَيْنات (عْوَيْناتات)
watch	*sē3a*	ساعة
earring	*ɧálʔa (ɧálaʔ)*	حلْقة (حلق)
ring	*xātim (xwētim)*	خاتِم (خْواتِم)
bracelet (solid)	*iswāra*	إسْوارة
bracelet (chain)	*[Fplaque]*	پْلاك
necklace	*3áʔid (3ʔūd)* *sinsēl*	عقِد (عْقود) سِنْسال
pendant	*[Fpendentif]* *ti3līʔa*	پانْدانْتيف تِعْليقة
silver	*fúḍḍa*	فُضّة
gold	*dáhab*	دهب

Expressions

Is there a larger size, please?	*fi ʔyēs ákbar, law samáɦit?*	في قْياس أكْبر لَوْ سمحِت؟
I would like this color too, please.	*báddi háyda -llōn kamēn, [please].*	بدّي هَيْدا اللّوْن كمان، پْليز.
This one has a small rip in it. Could I have another one?	*háyda fī xízi?, fīk ta3ţīni ɣáyru waláw?*	هَيْدا في خِزِق، فيك تعْطيني غَيْرو وَلَوْ؟
Can I try on both [pairs of shoes]?	*fíyi járrib ittnēn, 3mōl ma3rūf?*	فِيي جرِّب التّْنيْن، عْموْل معْروف؟
Is this local or Italian silver?	*háyda fúḍḍa šíɣil hōn aw ţilyēni/īţāli?*	هَيْدا فُضّة شِغِل هوْن أَوْ طِلْياني/إيطالي؟
How many karats is this gold?	*šū 3yāru háyda -ddáhab?*	شو عْيارو هَيْدا الدّهب؟
Do these glasses have a warranty?	*háwdi -l3waynēt 3aláyun kafēli?*	هَوْدي العْويْنات علَيْن كفالِة؟
I bought this pair of shoes from here and they tore apart the second time I wore them.	*štarēt háyda -lbōt/-ṣṣubbāţ min hōn, w nšáʔaf šaʔftēn min ba3d tēni lábsi!*	شْتريْت هَيْدا البوْت/ الصُّبّاط مِن هوْن، ونْشقف شقْفْتيْن مِن بعْد تاني لبْسِة!
Can I reserve this item until evening?	*fíyi íɦjuz háyda la-3ašíyyi?* *fīk txallīli háyda 3a jánab la-3ašíyyi?*	فِيي إحْجُز هَيْدا لعشية؟ فيك تْخلّيلي هَيْدا عَ جنب لعشية؟

Is there a smaller size at another branch?	*fī šī ʔyēs ázɣar bi-ɣēr fíri3?*	في شي قْياس أزْغر بغيرْ فرِع؟
Wow! That's a real bargain!	*wāw! háyda sí3ir bijánnin!* *wāw! sí3ir láʔṭa!*	واو! هَيْدا سِعِر بيجنِّن! واو! سِعِر لقْطة!

◇

This credit card is not working.	*háyda -k[credit card] miš mēši.* *háydi -lbiṭāʔa miš mēšyi.*	هَيْدا الكْرديت كرْد مِش ماشي. هَيْدي البِطاقة مِش ماشْيِة.
Returns are allowed within 30 days of the date of the sale, with a receipt.	*minrídd xilēl tlētīn yōm min tārīx ilbē3, bass lēzim ykūn má3ak ilwáṣil/ir[receipt].*	مِنرْدّ خِلال تْلاتين يوْم مِن تاريخ البيْع، بسّ لازِم يْكون معك الوَصِل/الرّيسيت.
There are no returns/refunds, but you can exchange it within 14 days.	*ma fīk tridd ʔúṭ3a štaráyta, bass fīk tbáddil xilēl arba3tá3šar yōm min tērīx ilbē3.*	ما فيك تْرِدّ قُطْعة شْترَيْتا، بسّ فيك تْبدِّل خِلال أرْبعْتعْشر يوْم مِن تاريخ البيْع.

At the Market بِالسّوق

أسْواق *aswēʔ* **markets** tell you a lot about a culture, and they're certainly a big part of the culture in Lebanon. Like markets around the world, those in Lebanon sell everything from تْياب *tyēb* **clothes** to بْهارات *bhārāt* **spices** and غْراض بيْت *ɣrād bēt* **things for the house**. Before malls took off just in the last decade or two, people did most of their shopping at the markets. They have lost some of their appeal to the novelty of malls, though some traditional markets, such as سوق الأحد *sūʔ il2áʔad* **Souq Al Ahad** (The Sunday Market) in Beirut and سوق العتيق *sūʔ il2atīʔ* (سوق القديم *sūʔ il2adīm*) **the Old Souq** in جْبيْل *jbēl* **Byblos**, remain the most affordable options. However, in the last few years, markets have started making a comeback with a new concept and look. أسْواق بيْروت *aswē2 bayrūt* **Beirut Souqs** and سوق الطّيِّب *sūʔ iṭṭáyyib* **Souq Al Tayeb** are definitely on the fancier end of the scale and have changed the image that traditional 'souqs' once had.

Buying a suitcase

o عفْواً، عم نبِّش[1] عَ شنْطِةْ سفر بِأرْبع دْواليب.

◇ هَوْدي التّْلات قْياسات اللي عِنّا ياهُن[2]. في قْماش وفي پْلاسْتيك.

o قدّيْ سِعْرا هَيْدي الزّْغيرِة الپْلاسْتيك؟

◇ خمْسين ألْف. وخفيفِة وضَيان.[3]

o Excuse me, I was looking for a suitcase with four wheels.

◇ Here are the three sizes available, some of which are fabric while others are plastic.

o How much is the small plastic one?

◇ 50,000 L.L. and it's light-weight and durable.

o *3áfwan, 3am nábbiš*[1] *3a šánṭit sáfar bi-árba3 dwēlīb.*

◇ *háwdi -ttlēt ʔyēsēt -lli 3ínna yēhun*[2]. *fī ʔmēš w fī [plastic].*

o *ʔaddē sí3ra háydi -zzɣīri -l[plastic]?*

◇ *xamsīn alf. w xafīfi w ḍayān.*[3]

[1] = فتِّش *fáttiš*

[2] = المِتْوَفّْرين *ilmitwaffrīn*

[3] خِدي الأكْبر. أغْلى بسّ عْلَيا كفالِةْ خمْس سْنين. *xídi -lʔákbar. áɣla bass 3láya kafēlit xams snīn.* **Buy the larger one. It's more expensive, but it has a five-year warranty.**

②

Buying cloth

o قدّيْ سِعْر المتِرْ مِنْ هَيْدا القِْماش؟
◇ المتِرْ بِعشرِْتلاف ليرة.
o إذا بدّي خيِّط بْلوزِة، قدّيْ بدّي قْماش قَوْلك[1]؟
◇ خِدي مِترْ ونُصّ. بيكفّيكي وزْيادِة.

o How much is a meter of this cloth?
◇ One meter is 10,000 L.L.
o If I wanted to make a skirt, how much would I need?
◇ Get one and a half meters. That will be plenty for you.

o *ʔaddē sí3r ilmítr min háyda -liʔmēš?*
◇ *-lmitr bi-3aširtalēf līra.*
o *íza báddi xáyyiṭ blūzi, ʔaddē báddi ʔmēš ʔáwlak*[1]*?*
◇ *xídi mítr w nuṣṣ. bikaffīki w zyēdi.*

[1] = قَوْلك *ʔáwlak* (lit. your say) **in your opinion**

3

Haggling (1)

○ قدّيْ سِعِر هالصّنية؟ ومِن شو معْمولِة[1]؟

◇ هَيْدي سْتانْلِس مدام، والمسْكات مْغطّسين[2] بِدهب. سِعْرا تمْانين ألْف ليرة.

○ لأ أكيد لأ. أسْعارك كْتير عالْيِة[3]. شِفْتا بمِحلّ تاني بِخمْسين ألْف.

◇ لحْظة. ما فِيي أعْطيكي ياها بْخمْسين. أكْتر شي فِيي أعْمِلّك إنّو أعْطيكي ياها بِخمْسة وسِتّين ألْف ليرة. وحْياتِك يَلّي شِفْتِيا بِهَيْداك السِّعِر مُسْتحيل تْكون ذات النَّوْعية[4].

○ How much is this tray? And what is it made from?

◇ This is stainless steel, ma'am, and the handles are gold-plated. It's 80,000 L.L.

○ No way! Your prices are too high. I've seen it in another shop for 50,000 L.L.!

◇ Hold on! I can't do 50,000 L.L. The best I can do is 65,000 L.L. Meet me halfway. I promise you the one that you've seen can't be the same quality for that price.

○ *ʔaddē sí3ir ha-ṣṣaníyyi? w min šū ma3mūli[1]?*

◇ *háydi [stainless], [F madame], w ilmaskēt mɣaṭṭasīn[2] bi-dáhab. sí3ra tmēnīn alf līra.*

○ *laʔ, akīd laʔ. as3ārak ktīr 3ālyi[3]. šífta bi-maḫáll tēni bi-xamsīn alf.*

◇ *láḫẓa. ma fíyi a3ṭīki yēha bi-xamsīn. áktar šī fíyi a3míllik ínnu a3ṭīki yēha bi-xámsa w sittīn alf līra. w ḫyētik yálli šiftíya bi-haydēk issí3ir mustaḫīl tkūn zēt innaw3íyyi[4].*

[1] = مصْنوعة *maṣnū3a*

[2] = مِطْلِيّين *miṭliyyīn*

[3] = مْبالغة *mbālaɣa* **exaggerated**

[4] أكيد تِقْليد *akīd tiʔlīd* **surely counterfeit**

4

Haggling (2)

o كْتير غالْيين هَوْدي. قدّيْ أرْخص شي فِيي آخِدُن؟
◇ بسّ إلِك، بعْطيكي ياهُن بِخمْسْتلاف القُطْعة[1].
o أوْكي رح آخُد سبْعة فإذاً بِخمْسة وتْلاتين ألْف ليرة.[2]
◇ أوْكي مبْروك! بِتْحِبّي لِفِّلِك ياهُن؟
o أيْه پْليز لِفّيلي ياهُن ع ذَوْقِك پْليز.

o But this is really expensive. What's the least I can get it for?
◇ Just for you, I will give it to you for 5,000 L.L. a piece.
o Okay, I'll take seven for 35,000 L.L. then.
◇ Okay, congratulations! Would you like me to wrap them for you?
o Yes, wrap them up nicely for me.

o *ktīr ɣālyīn háwdi. ʔaddē árxaṣ šī fíyi ēxidun?*
◇ *bass ílik, ba3ṭīki yēhun bi-xámstalēf ilʔúṭ3a*[1].
o *okē, raḫ ēxud sáb3a fa-ízan bi-xámsa w tlētīn alf līra.*[2]
◇ *okē, mabrūk! bitḫíbbi liffílik yēhun?*
o *ē, [please] liffīli yēhun 3a záwʔik, [please].*

[1] = الوحْدِة *ilwíḫdi*

[2] إذا باخُد أكْتر مِن وِحْدِة، بْتعْمِلّي سِعِر؟ *íza bēxud áktar min wíḫdi, bta3mílli sí3ir.*
If I buy more than one, will you give me a good price?

5

Turning down a salesperson

○ فوتي وتْفرّجي عَ كِلّ الإشْيا الأثرية اللي عِنّا ياهُن.
◇ لأ مرْسي، منّي عايْزِة شي.
○ تْفرّجي بسّ. ما رح تْلاقي مِتِل أسْعارْنا غيْر مطْرح.[1]
◇ ما بدّي إشْترْي شي أصْلاً. مرْسي![2]

◇ Come on in, and have a look at the antiques we've got.
○ Thank you, I don't want any.
◇ Just take a look. You won't find prices like these [anywhere else].
○ I don't want to buy anything anyway. Thanks!

○ *fūti w tfarráji 3a kill ilʔíšya -lʔasaríyyi -lli 3ínna yēhun.*
◇ *laʔ [ᶠmerci], mánni 3āyzi šī.*
○ *tfarráji bass. ma raḫ tlēʔi mítil as3ārna ɣēr máṭraḫ.*[1]
◇ *ma báddi íštri šī áṣlan. [ᶠmerci]!*[2]

[1] أسْعارْنا مدْروسِة *as3ārna madrūsi* **our prices are researched** (i.e. we took care to set the best prices)

[2] شُكْراً، مِش جايي إشْترْي. *šúkran, miš jēyi íštri.*

6

Paying

○ أوْكي، قدّيْ بدّك مِنّي؟[1]

◇ كِلُّن سَوا بْيِطْلعوا[2] تْلاتّعْشر ألْف ليرة.

○ ما معي إلّا عشرْتلاف بِاللِّبْناني. وَإلّا بيصير بدّك تِصْرُفْلي عِشْرين دوْلار.

◇ لحْظة، خلّيني شوف إذا حدا مْن المحلّات اللي حدّي معُن صْرافِة للعِشْرين دوْلار.[3]

○ ولك يَلّا، خْصوم التْلاتّلاف يا مْعلِّم.

◇ أوْكيْ مدام. ألْف مبْروك.

○ Okay, so how much do I owe you?

◇ All together, that will be 13,000 L.L.

○ I only have 10,000 L.L. in L.L. Otherwise, you'll have to break a $20.

◇ Wait, let me see if any of the neighboring shops have any change for $20.

○ Come on, just waive the 3,000 L.L., sir!

◇ Okay, ma'am. Enjoy!

○ *okē, ʔaddē báddak mínni?*[1]

◇ *kíllun sáwa byíṭla3u*[2] *tlēttá3šar alf līra.*

○ *ma má3i ílla 3aširtalēf bi-llibnēni. wa-ílla biṣīr báddak tiṣrúfli 3išrīn dólar.*

◇ *láħẓa, xallīni šūf íza ħáda mn ilmaħallēt -lli ħáddi má3un ṣrāfi la-l3išrīn dólar.*[3]

○ *w lak yálla, xṣūm ittlēttalēf ya m3állim.*

◇ *okē, [ᶠmadame]. alf mabrūk.*

[1] = قدّيْ بِتْريد؟ *ʔaddē bitrīd?* / [2] = مجْموعُن *majmū3un* / [3] خلص لكان، هاتي عشْرة. *xálaṣ lakēn, hēti 3áśra.* **No problem, then. Give me 10[,000 L.L.].**

○ بدّي آخُد[1] هْدية حِلْوِة لإمّي مِن لِبْنان.

◇ عِنْدي كْتير إشْيا حِلْوِة. عِنْدي جْزادين عْلَيا العلم اللِّبْناني، وكوْليفيشيْه، وتكّايات.

○ بْتحِبّ الإشْيا اللي شِغِل إيد. حابّة شي فِيا تْعلّقو عالحيْط.

◇ شو رأْيِك بِهَيْدا؟

○ عن شو بْتِحْكي[2] الكتيبِة اللي عْليْه؟

◇ هَيْدي مْن النّشيد الوَطني اللّبْناني.

○ الألْوان بِيعقّدوا[3]! شو بْتْقول عالمظْبوط؟

◇ أوّل جِمْلِة مْن النّشيد الوَطني: "كُلُّنا لِلوَطن لِلعُلى لِلعلم."

○ اه! كْتير حِلْوِة الفِكْرة. رح تْحِبّو كْتير. عِنْدك ياه بِغيرْ ألْوان، إذا بدّي آخُد أكْتر مِن واحد.

◇ في هَيْدا بْتِجي خلْفيتو كِتّان. وفي القْماش العادي عِنْدي مِنّو عِدِّةْ ألْوان.

○ قدّيْ سِعْر الكِتّان؟

◇ الكِتّان بِعِشْرين ألْف. والقْماش العادي تْمانْتعْشر ألْف ليرة.

○ أوْكيْ فِيي آخد تْنيْن كِتّان بِتْلاتين ألْف؟

◇ صدّقيني ما بْتْوَفّي.[4]

○ بْرْجع بِكِلّ فُرْصة، وبِبْعت كِلّ أصْحابي لعِنْدِك. پْليز عْمْليلي سِعِر مْنيح.

◇ فِيي أعْطيكي التّْنيْن بِخمْسة وتْلاتين ألْف، بسّ والله ما فِيي أكْتر مِن هيْك[5].

○ طيِّب أوْكيْ، بسّ پْليز لِفّيلي ياهُن عَ ذَوْقِك.

◇ تِكْرم عَيْنِك!

- o I want to get a really nice gift from Lebanon for my mom.
- ◇ I have lots of nice things: purses with the Lebanese flag, knick-knacks, cushions...
- o Well, she really likes hand-made fabric decorations. I'd like something she can hang on the wall.
- ◇ How about this?
- o What does the writing on it say?
- ◇ It's from the Lebanese National Anthem on embroidered, patchwork cloth.
- o The colors are really beautiful. What does it say exactly?
- ◇ It's just the first verse of the national anthem. It says "All of us! For our Country, for our Glory and Flag!"
- o Ah, that's a really good idea. She'll really like it, but do you have it in other colors, so I can take more than one?
- ◇ There is this one on a linen background and another one on regular fabric in different colors.
- o Well, the linen one is better. How much is it then?
- ◇ The linen one is 20,000 L.L., and the regular fabric one is 18,000 L.L.
- o I will take two linen ones for 30,000 L.L.
- ◇ Believe me, I can't do that.
- o I'll come back on every holiday, and I'll refer my friends to you, so please give me a really good price.
- ◇ I'll give you both for 35,000 L.L., and that's really my final offer.
- o Okay fine. Just please wrap them nicely for me.
- ◇ My pleasure!

- o *báddi ēxud[1] hdíyyi ɧílwi la-ímmi min libnēn.*
- ◇ *3índi ktīr íšya ɧílwi. 3índi jzēdīn 3láya -l3álam illibnēni, w [F colifichets], w takkēyēt.*
- o *bitɧíbb ilʔíšya -lli šíɣil īd. ɧābbi šī fíya t3állʔu 3a-lɧēṭ.*
- ◇ *šū ráʔyik bi-háyda?*

- ○ *3an šū btíɧki*[2] *-lkatībi -lli 3lē?*
- ◇ *háydi mn innašīd ilwáʈani -llibnēni.*
- ○ *-lʔalwēn bi3áʔʔdu*[3]*! šū bitʔūl 3a-lmaʐbūʈ?*
- ◇ *áwwal jímli mn innašīd ilwaʈáni: "kullúna li-lwáʈan li-l3úla li-l3álam."*
- ○ *āh! ktīr ɧílwi -lfíkra. raɧ tɧíbbu ktīr. 3índak yēh bi-ɣēr alwēn, íza báddi ēxud áktar min wāɧad.*
- ◇ *fī háyda btíji xalfīytu kittēn. w fī -liʔmēš il3ādi 3índi mínnu 3íddit alwēn.*
- ○ *ʔaddē sí3r ilkittēn?*
- ◇ *-lkittēn bi-3išrīn alf. w liʔmēš il3ādi tmēntá3šar alf līra.*
- ○ *okē, fíyi ēxud tnēn kittēn bi-tlētīn alf?*
- ◇ *ʂaddʔīni ma bitwáffi.*[4]
- ○ *bírja3 bi-kíll fúrʂa, w bíb3at kill aʂɧābi la-3índik. [please], 3mlīli sí3ir mnīɧ.*
- ◇ *fíyi a3ʈīki -ttnēn bi-xámsa w tlētīn alf, bass wálla ma fíyi áktar min hēk*[5]*.*
- ○ *ʈáyyib okē, bass [please] liffīli yēhun 3a záwʔik.*
- ◇ *tíkram 3áynik!*

[1] = إشْتْري *íštri*

[2] = شو معْنى *šū má3na* **what's the meaning of...**

[3] بيعقّدوا *bi3áʔʔdu* (lit. they give me a complex) as in, they're 'so beautiful that they give me a complex (make me go crazy), a common expression.

[4] تِكْرِم عَيْنِك. بسّ كِرْمال نِكْسبِك زْبونة. *tíkram 3áynik. bass kirmēl níksabik zbūni.* **As you wish, but just to keep you as a customer.**

[5] = هَيْدا آخِر عرِض *háyda ēxir 3áriɖ*

Vocabulary

market	*sū? (aswē?)*	سوق (أسْواق)
price	*sí3ir (as3ār)*	سِعِر (أسْعار)
haggling	*msēwami 3a-ssí3ir* *šarī3a 3a-ssí3ir*	مْساوَمِة عالسِّعِر شريعة عالسِّعِر
wrapping	*laff (yliff)*	لفّ (يْلِفّ)
plastic bag	*kīs (kyēs)*	كيس (كْياس)
fabric, cloth	*?mēš*	قْماش
cotton	*?úţun*	قُطُن
wool	*şūf*	صوف
linen	*kittēn*	كِتّان
silk	*ɦarīr*	حرير
dress	*fisţān (fasāţīn)*	فِسْطان (فساطين)
fez	*ţarbūš*	طرْبوش
flip-flops	*miššēyi (b-íşba3)*	مِشّايِة (بإصْبع)
headscarf	*ɦjēb*	حْجاب
scarf	*šēl*	شيْل
(natural) leather	*jild (ţabī3i)*	جِلْد (طبيعي)
decorative object, nick-nack; antique	*tíɦfi (tíɦaf)*	تِحْفِة (تِحف)
marble	*rxām*	رْخام
pearl	*lūlu*	لولو
copper	*nɦās*	نْحاس

silver	*fúḍḍa*	فُضّة
gold	*dáhab*	دهب
tray	*ṣaníyyi*	صنية
keychain	*[[F]porte-clés]*	پوْرْت كْليْه
glass, cup	*kibbēyi*	كِبّايِة
plate	*ṣáɦin (ṣɦūn)*	صحِن (صْحون)
cushion	*mxáddi* *takkēyi*	مْخدِّة تكّايِة
beads	*xáraz*	خرز
thread	*xēṭ (xyūṭ)*	خيْط (خْيوط)
doll	*[[F]poupée]* *lí3bi*	پوپيْه لِعْبِة
camel	*jámal (jmēl)*	جمل (جْمال)
lantern	*fēnūs*	فانوس
loofah	*līfi*	ليفِة
local/organic soap	*ṣābūn báladi*	صابون بلدي
ambergris (a natural perfume substance)	*3ánbar*	عنْبر
mint	*ná3na3*	نعْنع
edible seeds (sun-flower, pumpkin...)	*bízir*	بْذِر
olive oil	*zēt zaytūn*	زيْت زَيْتون
date syrup	*díbis támir*	دِبِس تمِر

Expressions

What is this, please?	*šū háyda, law samáħit?*	شو هَيْدا لَوْ سمحِت؟
How much is this?	*ʔaddē háyda?*	قدّيْ هَيْدا؟
Was this made in China or Lebanon?	*háyda šíɣl iṣṣīn aw libnēn?*	هَيْدا شِغْل الصّين أَوْ لِبْنان؟
Please, tell me the total of these separately from those.	*[please], ʔílli ʔaddē háwdi la-ħāl w háwdi la-ħāl?* *[please], ʔílli ʔaddē si3r kill wāħad la-ħāl?*	پْليز قِلّي قدّيْ هَوْدي لحال وهَوْدي لحال؟ پْليز قِلّي قدّيْ سِعْر كِلّ واحد لحال؟
Well, if I buy 10, how much will it cost me?	*íza štarēt 3ášra, ʔaddē byíṭla3u?*	إذا شْتريْت عشْرة، قدّيْ بْيِطْلعوا؟
(haggling) Give me a good discount then.	*3míli xáṣim 3a záwʔak fa-ízan.*	عْمِلي خصِم عَ ذَوْقك فإذاً.
Weigh out three separate half-kilos of raisins for me.	*3mōl ma3rūf, zínli tlēt kyēs zbīb kill nuṣṣ kīlu wáħdu/ la-ħāl.*	عْموْل معْروف زِنْلي تْلات كْياس زْبيب كِلّ نُصّ كيلو وَحْدو/ لحال.
Cut two meters of this cloth for me, please.	*law samáħit, ʔíṣṣli mitrēn min háyda liʔmēš.*	لَوْ سمحِت، قِصّْلي مِتْريْن مِن هَيْدا القْماش.
Can you please wrap each separately?	*3mōl ma3rūf, bitlíffilli kill wíħdi wáħda?*	عْموْل معْروف، بِتْلِفِّلّي كِلّ وِحْدِة وَحْدا؟
(looking for a stall's merchant) Is there anyone here?	*fī ħáda hōn?*	في حدا هوْن؟

This type of cloth is one-sided [not double-sided] and one meter costs 5,000 L.L.	*nō3 liʔmēš háyda miš [ᶠdouble face], w -lmitr bi-xamstalēf līra.*	نوْع القْماش هَيْدا مِش دوبْل فاس، والمِترْ بِخمْسْتلاف ليرة.
(responding to haggling) This won't work for me.	*ma bitwáffi má3i.*	ما بِتْوَفّي معي.
No haggling. That's the final price.	*bála šarī3a 3a-ssí3ir. háyda ēxir sí3ir.*	بلا شريعة عالسِّعِر. هَيْدا آخِر سِعِر.
(about a neigh-boring merchant) Just wait a second and the merchant there will come back.	*nṭūr sawēni bass, w byíji -lbayyē3.*	نْطور ثَواني بسّ، وبْيِجي البيّاع.

At a Hotel

بِالأوْتيْل

The Lebanese are known for their ضْيافِة *ḍyāfi* **hospitality**, so, naturally, أوْتيْلات *[ᶠhôtel]ēt* **hotels** are a big deal and pride themselves for excellent hospitality. That said, hotels' star ratings don't always seem to reflect what you might expect. This is especially true of local, independent hotels–and the further away you get from major cities, the more exaggerated the star ratings tend to be. Hotels seem to self-rate themselves and take into consideration not only the hotels' amenitites but also consider the rating inclusive of the location and access to attractions. Unless you already have a حجِز *ḥájiz* **reservation**, you'll have to ask if there are any أُوَض فاضْيِة *úwaḍ fāḍyi* **vacancies** at the ريسيپْشَن *[receptoion]* **front desk**.

○ لَوْ سمحْتي. هلّق بعْدْني جايي مْن المطار وكان بدّي شوف إذا عِنْدْكُن أُوَض فاضْيِة.
◇ أهْلا وسهْلا مونْسْيور. ثَواني بسّ وبْشِفْلك.[1]
○ أيْه پْليز. بدّي بسّ لَيْلْتينْ[2] تكْنِت ظبّطِت أموري.
◇ أوْكيْ إسْتاذ، في عِنّا أوضة بمِية وخمْسين دوْلار بِاللَّيْلِة مع تِرْويقة.[3]
○ تمام. حْجِزيلي ياها ليْلْتين پْليز.[4]

○ Excuse me, I just arrived from the airport, and I was wondering if there are any rooms available?
◇ Welcome, sir! Just a moment and I'll take a look for you.
○ Yes, please. I only need two nights, until I get everything settled.
◇ Okay, sir, there is a room available for $150 a night and includes breakfast.
○ Excellent. Book it for me for two nights, please.

○ *law samáħti. hálla? bá3dni jēyi mn ilmaṭār w kēn báddi šūf íza 3índkun úwaḍ fāḍyi.*
◇ *áhla w sáhla, [^F monsieur]. sawēni bass w bšíflak.*[1]
○ *ē, [please]. báddi bass layltēn*[2] *ta-kínit ẓabbáṭit umūri.*
◇ *okē istēz, fī 3ínna ūḍa bi-míyyi w xamsīn dólar bi-lláyli ma3 tirwī?a.*[3]
○ *tamēm. ħjizīli yēha layltēn, [please].*[4]

[1] = شرِّفِت إِسْتاز. خلّيني إتْأَكّدْلك. *šarráfit, istēz. xallīni it?akkádlak.*

[2] = بسّ عْلى يَوْمينْ *bass 3la yawmēn*

[3] في عِنّا غِرْفِة مع فْطور مِتْوَفْرة. *fī 3ínna ɣírfi ma3 fṭūr mitwáffra.* **We have a room with breakfast available.**

[4] مُمْتاز. عْطيني ياها عْلى يَوْمينْ. *mumtēz. 3ṭīni yēha 3la yawmēn.*

2

Checking In

○ لَوْ سمحْتي، عِنْدي حجِز بِإِسِم سارة عيد.

◇ بسّ ثَواني، تإتْأكّد مْن الحجِز. مظْبوط، حجزْتي أوضة سينْجِل مع تِرْويقة[1].

○ صحّ. وحجزِت الأوضة يَلّي معا بالْكوْن[2] پْليز.

◇ مظْبوط، أوْكيْ. بِتْحِبّي الأوضة يَلّي بِتْطِلّ عالبحِر؟ أَوْ يَلّي بِتْطِلّ عالجبل؟[3]

○ لأ بْفضِّل يَلّي بِتْطِلّ عالبحِر، پْليز.

◇ أوْكيْ، مدام. بدّي پاسْپوْرِك والكْرديت كارْد تبعِك لَوْ سمحْتي.[4]

○ Hi, I have a room booked under the name Sarah Eid.

◇ Just a moment. I'll double-check... Yes, that's correct. You've booked a single room with breakfast.

○ Exactly. And I booked one with a balcony, please.

◇ Correct. All right, would you prefer the room overlooking the sea or the mountains?

○ No, I'd rather have one overlooking the sea, please.

◇ All right, ma'am. Could I have your passport and credit card, please?

○ *law samáɧti, 3índi ɧájiz bi-ísim [Sarah] 3īd.*

◇ *bass sawēni, ta-it?ákkad mn ilɧájiz. maẓbūṭ, ɧajázti ūḍa [single] ma3 tirwī?a[1].*

○ *ṣaɧɧ. w ɧajázit il?ūḍa yálli má3a [Fbulcon][2], [please].*

◇ *maẓbūṭ, okē. bitɧíbbi -l?ūḍa yálli bitṭíll 3a-lbáɧir? aw yálli bitṭíll 3a-ljábal?[3]*

○ *la? bfáḍḍil yálli bitṭíll 3a-lbáɧir, [please].*

◇ *okē, [Fmadame]. báddi paspōrik w il[credit card] tába3ik, law samáɧti.[4]*

[1] = فْطور *fṭūr* / [2] = شِرْفِة *šírfi* / [3] بِتْحِبِّي غِرْفِة مع مْطلّ؟ *bitɧíbbi ɣírfi ma3 mṭall?* **Do you want a room with a view?** / [4] = تمام. عْطيني پاسْپوْرِك و بِطاقْتِك عْمِلي معْروف. *tamēm. 3ṭīni paspōrik w biṭā?tik, 3míli ma3rūf.*

3

Arriving in your room

o فيك پْليز تْحُطّ الشِّنط حِدّ[1] الخْزانِة؟
◇ أكيد إسْتاذ. يَحِنِّ حدّ الخْزانِة. وهَيْدا مِفْتاح الأوضِة[2].
o أوْكي مرْسي كْتير. فيك كمان تعْطيني رقْم الرّيسيپْشُن عْمول معْروف؟[3]
◇ بْتْدِقّ عالصِّفِر، وبْتِتْحوّل عالرّيسيپْشْن. هِنِّ بيساعْدوك إذا بدّك حيّالله شي.[4]

o Could you put the luggage next to the wardrobe?
◇ Yes, sir... The luggage is beside the wardrobe. Here's the room key.
o Okay, thank you very much. Would you please tell me the number for the reception?
◇ You press zero, and you'll be connected to the reception. They will assist you if you need anything.

o *fīk [please] tħuṭṭ iššínaṭ ħadd[1] lixzēni?*
◇ *akīd istēz. yaħínni ħadd lixzēni. w háyda miftēħ ilʔūḍa[2].*
o *okē [Fmerci] ktīr. fīk kamēn ta3ṭīni ráʔm ir[reception], 3mōl ma3rūf?[3]*
◇ *bitdíʔʔ 3a-ṣṣífir, w btitħáwwal 3a-r[reception]. hínni bisē3dūk íza báddak ħayyálla šī.[4]*

1 = جنْب *jamb*

2 = الغِرْفِة *ilɣírfi*

3 = يِسْلمو. فيك تعْطيني نُمْرِةْ الإسْتِقْبال إذا بترْيد. *yíslamu. fīk ta3ṭīni númrit ilʔistiʔbēl, íza bitrīd.*

4 = بْتِتّصِل عالزّيرو. أيّا خِدْمِة هِنِّ تحِت أمْرك. *btittíṣil 3a-z[zero]. áyya xídmi hínni táħit ámrak.* **Dial zero. They're at your service.**

4

Calling the front desk

o بدّي منْشفِة للبحِر، پْليز. ما لْقيت وَلا وِحْدة بِالحمّام.

◇ المناشِف عالبحِر دُمْوازيْل. فيكي تاخْدي وِحْدِة إذا بِتْفرْجين الكي كارْد تبعِك.

o اه أوْكي. وبدّي كمان منْشفِة لأوضْتي، پْليز.[1]

◇ أيْه أكيد دُمْوازيْل. خمْس دقايِق وبِتْكون عِنْدِك.[2]

o أوْكي، مرْسي كْتير. وپْليز إذا فيكي كمان تْدِقّيلّي عالغرْفِة خمْستعْش.[3]

o I'd like a towel for the beach, please. I couldn't find any in the bathroom.

◇ Towels can be found at the beach. You can check one out using your key card.

o Ah, okay. I also need an extra towel in my room, please.

◇ Yes, miss, of course. You'll have one in just five minutes.

o All right, thanks a lot. Also, please, connect me to room 15.

o *báddi mánšafi la-lbáɦir, [please]. ma lʔīt wála wíɦdi bi-lɦammēm.*

◇ *-lmanēšif 3a-lbáɦir, [Fdemoiselle]. fīki tēxdi wíɦdi íza bitfarjíyun il[key card] tába3ik.*

o *āh okē. w báddi kamēn mánšafi la-ūḍti, [please][1].*

◇ *ē, akīd, [Fdemoiselle]. xams dʔāyiʔ w bitkūn 3indik.[2]*

o *okē, [Fmerci] ktīr. w [please] íza fīki kamēn tdiʔʔīlli 3a-lɣírfi xamstá3š.[3]*

[1] = عْمِلي معْروف *3míli ma3rūf* = إذا بِتْريدي *íza bitrīdi*

[2] تِكْرم عْيونِك، هلّق مْنِبْعتْلِك وِحْدِة. *tíkram 3yūnik, hállaʔ mnib3átlik wíɦdi.* **At your service. We'll send one up right away.**

[3] = يِسْلمو. مُمْكِن تْحوّْليني عالْغرْفِة خمْستعْش؟ *yíslamu. múmkin tɦawwlīni 3a-lɣírfi xamstá3š?* **Thank you. Can you connect me to room 15?**

5

Asking to Change Rooms

- ○ بدّي غيرّ أوضْتي پْليز.
- ◇ أكيد دْمْوازيْل. فِيي إِسْأل لِيْه؟[1]
- ○ كان مفْروض الأوضة تْطِلّ عالبحِر بسّ ما فِيي شوف البحِر لأِنّو البِنايات مْغطّيْتْلي الڤْيو.[2]
- ◇ أوْكيْ دْمْوازيْل. فينا نِنْقلِك عَ أوضة بِطابِق أعْلى.[3]
- ○ أيْه پْليز. مرْسي كْتير.[4]

- ○ I'd like to change rooms, please.
- ◇ Certainly, miss. May I know the reason?
- ○ It's supposed to be a room overlooking the sea, but I cannot see anything because of the buildings.
- ◇ Okay, miss. We can move you to a room on an upper floor.
- ○ Yes, please. Thanks so much!

- ○ *báddi ɣáyyir ūḍti, [please].*
- ◇ *akīd, [Fdemoiselle]. fíyi ísʔal lē?*[1]
- ○ *kēn mafrūḍ ilʔūḍa tṭill 3a-lbáħir bass ma fíyi šūf ilbáħir li-ánnu -lbinēyēt mɣáṭṭyitli -l[view].*[2]
- ◇ *okē, [Fdemoiselle]. fīna nínʔilik 3a ūḍa bi-ṭābiʔ á3la.*[3]
- ○ *ē, [please]. [Fmerci] ktīr.*[4]

[1] = فِيي أعْرِف شو السّبب؟ *fíyi á3rif šū -ssábab?*

[2] المكيِّف خرْبان ما عم يْبرِّد. *-lmukáyyif xarbēn ma 3am ybárrid.* **The air conditioner is broken and isn't putting out cool air.**

[3] بِعْتِزِر مِنّك، كِلّ الغِرف مْفوْلين. هلّق بِبْعتْلِك عامل الصِّيانِة يِكْشِف عْليْه. *bi3tízir mínnik, kill ilɣíraf mfáwwlīn. hállaʔ bib3átlik 3āmil iṣṣiyēni yíkšif 3lē.* **I apologize. All of the rooms are full. I will send you the maintenance technician to check on it right away.**

[4] = أيْ، إذا بِتْريد. شُكْراً *ē, íza bitrīd. šúkran.*

6

Asking about breakfast

o فيكي تْقوليلي أَوْقات التِّرْويقة[1] پْليز؟

◇ التِّرْويقة بِالمطْعم مْن السِّتّة الصُّبُح لِلحْدعْش الصُّبُح. بوفيْه مفْتوح.

o أوْكي. في مجال تْطلّعولي الأكِل عالأوضة؟

◇ لِلأسف إسْتاذ ما فينا نْطلِّع أكِل مْن البوفيْه عالأوضة. عِنّا مينْو تِرْويقة تاني لِلضّيوف يَلّي بيحِبّوا يِترْوّقوا بِغِرفُن[2]. بسّ هَيْدا منّو مشْمول بِسِعْر الغِرْفة اللي حضِرْتك دفعْتو.

o Can I find out the times for breakfast?

◇ Breakfast is in the restaurant from 6:00am until 11:00am. It's an open buffet.

o All right. Is it possible to have it delivered to my room?

◇ Unfortunately, it will not be possible to deliver buffet items to the room, sir. We do have a separate breakfast menu for in-room dining, but that is a separate cost and is not included in your booking.

o *fīki tʔūlīli awʔāt ittirwīʔa*[1]*, [please]?*

◇ *-ttirwīʔa bi-lmáṭ3am mn issítti -ṣṣúbuḫ la-liḫdá3š iṣṣúbuḫ. būfē maftūḫ.*

o *okē. fī majēl tṭall3ūli -lʔákil 3a-lʔūḍa?*

◇ *li lʔásaf istēz, ma fīna nṭálli3 ákil mn ilbūfē 3a-lʔūḍa. 3inna [menu] tirwīʔa tēni la-ḍḍyūf yálli biḫíbbu yitráwwaʔu bi-ɣírafun*[2]*. bass háyda mánnu mašmūl bi-sí3r ilɣírfi -lli ḫáḍirtak dafá3tu.*

[1] = الفْطور *lifṭūr*

[2] (lit. for guests who want to eat in their rooms)

o بدّي أوضة سينْجِل عَ تْلات لَيالي پْليز.

◇ في شي حجز بِإسْمِك مادام؟

o لِلأسف لأ. حجزت أونْلايْن بسّ كان في مِشْكْلِة ومنّي مِتْأكّدِة إذا ظبط الحجز أَوْ لأ.

◇ أوْكيْ، خلّيني شِفْلِك. مْمْ... فِيي شوف الپاسْپوْرْ پْليز؟

o تْفضّلي، حجزْتو مِن جِمِعْتيْن، بسّ اليوْم بسّ رِحِت عالوَبْسايْت، ما لْقيت وَلا شي عن الحجِز.

◇ لِلأسف الحجِز ما تْأكّد، بسّ خلّيني شِفْلِك. إذا في عِنّا أُوَض فاضْيِة بِذات الْمواصفات.

o أيْه إذا بِتْريدي. كْتير ضروري. بسّ عَ تْلات لَيالي.

◇ أوْكيْ في أوضة أقيْلِبِل بسّ ما بِتْطِلّ عالبحِر.

o فِيا بالْكوْن؟

◇ هِيِّ أوضة جنابية فِيا بالْكوْن بِتْطِلّ عالجبل.

o أوْكيْ ما في مشْكل. حْجِزيلي ياها پْليز.

◇ أوْكيْ هَوْدي المفاتيح تبع الأوضة، شِنطِك بيطلّعولِك ياهُن عَ أوضْتِك.

o أوْكيْ، وبدّي خريطة لبَيْروت إذا في مجال، تاقْدر روح وإجي.

◇ أكيد مادام. هَيْدي خريطة عْلَيا كِلّ المحلّات الأثرية الْمِهِمِّة وأرْقام تِلِفوْنات شرْكات تاكْسي ومعْلومات عن النّقْل العامّ.

o أوْكيْ وشو رقْم الرّسيبْشِن، لَوْ سمحْتي.

◇ إذا عِزْتي حَيّالله شي، إتِّصْلي بِصِفِر صِفِر للرّسيبْشِن.

o أوْكيْ وشو پاسْوورْد الوَيْفَيْ؟

◇ مَوْجود عَ وَرْقة حدّ التِّلِفوْن بِأوضْتِك.

o أوْكي مرْسي كْتير!
◇ أهْلا وسهْلا مادام. انْشالله يْكون وَقْتِك عِنّا عَ ذَوْقِك.

o I need a single room for three nights, please.
◇ Did you book in advance under your name, ma'am?
o Unfortunately, I made the reservation online, but there was some problem, and I'm not sure if it really got booked or not.
◇ Okay, let me check for you. Could I have your passport?
o Here you are. I booked it about two weeks ago, but today I checked the website and couldn't find any details on the reservation.
◇ Unfortunately, the reservation was not confirmed, but let me check for you if there are any available rooms with the same preferences.
o Yes, please. Just for three nights. It's urgent.
◇ All right, there is a room available, but it doesn't overlook the sea directly.
o Is there a balcony?
◇ It's a side room with a balcony overlooking the mountains.
o Okay, no problem. Book it for me, please.
◇ Okay, here are the keys. The luggage will be brought to you upstairs.
o All right. And I needed a city map for getting around, if possible.
◇ Certainly, ma'am. Here's a map with the key touristic sights, cab company numbers, and information about public transport.
o Okay. And what is the number for the reception, please?
◇ If you need anything at all, just dial 00 for the reception.
o Okay, and how about the wifi password?

◇ It's on a piece of paper next to the telephone in your room.

○ All right, thanks a lot!

◇ You're welcome, ma'am. We hope your stay with us is a pleasant one!

○ *báddi ūḑa [single] 3a tlēt layēli, [please].*

◇ *fī šī ɧájiz bi-ísmik, [^{F}madame]?*

○ *li-lʔásaf laʔ. ɧájazit [online] bass kēn fī míškli w mánni mitʔákkdi íza ẓábaţ ilɧájiz aw laʔ.*

◇ *okē, xallīni šíflik. mmm... fíyi šūf ilpaspōr, [please]?*

○ *tfáḑḑali, ɧajáztu min jimi3tēn, bass ilyōm bass ríɧit 3a-l[website], ma lʔīt wála šī 3an ilɧájiz.*

◇ *li-lʔásaf, ilɧájiz ma tʔákkad, bass xallīni šíflik íza fī 3ínna úwaḑ fāḑyi bi-zēt ilmuwāşafēt.*

○ *ē, íza bitrīdi. ktīr ḑarūri. bass 3a tlēt layēli.*

◇ *okē fī ūḑa [available] bass ma bitţíll 3a-lbáɧir.*

○ *fíya [^{F}balcon]?*

◇ *híyyi ūḑa janēbíyyi fíya [^{F}balcon] bitţíll 3a-ljábal.*

○ *okē ma fī máškal. ɧjizīli yēha, [please].*

◇ *okē háwdi -lmafātīɧ tába3 ilʔūḑa, w šínaţik biţall3ūlik yēhun 3a ūḑtik.*

○ *okē, w báddi xarīţa la-bayrūt íza fī majēl, ta-íʔdar rūɧ w íji.*

◇ *akīd, [^{F}madame]. háydi xarīţa 3láya kill ilmaɧallēt ilʔasaríyyi limhímmi w arʔām [^{F}téléphone]ēt širkēt táksi w ma3lūmēt 3an innáʔl il3āmm.*

○ *okē w šū ráʔm ir[reception], law samáɧti.*

◇ *íza 3ízti ɧayyálla šī, ittíşli bi-şífir şífir la-r[reception].*

○ *okē w šū [password] il[wifi]?*

◇ *mawjūd 3a wárʔa ɧadd it[^{F}téléphone] bi-ūḑtik.*

○ *okē [^{F}merci] ktīr!*

◇ *áhla w sáhla, [^{F}madame]. nšálla ykūn wáʔtik 3ínna 3a záwʔik.*

Vocabulary

hotel	[[F]hôtel] fínduʔ (fanēdiʔ)	أوْتيْل فِنْدُق (فنادِق)
lobby	[[F]corridor]	كوْريدوْر
reception	[reception] istiʔbēl	ريسيپْشُن اِسْتِقْبال
reservation, booking	ħájiz	حجِز
confirmation	taʔkīd ħájiz	تأْكيد حجِز
credit card	[credit card]	كْريْدِت كارْد
cash	[cash]	كاش
room key	miftēħ ūḍa	مِفْتاح أوضة
room card	[[F]carte] ūḍa	كارْت أوضة
single room	ūḍa [single]	أوضة سينْجِل
double room	ūḍa [double]	أوضة دابِل
suite	[[F]suite] jnēħ	سْويت جْناح
half board, with breakfast and dinner	tirwīʔa w 3áša	تِرْويقة وعشا
full board, with three meals a day	tirwīʔa w ɣáda w 3áša	تِرْويقة وغدا وعشا
full board, with three meals a day	[full board]	فول بوْرْد
balcony	[[F]balcon]	بلْكوْن
a room facing the sea	ūḍa baħríyyi ūḍa mwējha -lbáħir	أوضة بحْرية

	ūḍa bitṭúll 3a-lbáɦir	أوضة مْواجْهة البحِر أوضة بِتْطُلّ عالبحِر
a room facing the mountains	*ūḍa mwējha -ljábal* *ūḍa bitṭúll 3a-ljábal*	أوضة مْواجْهة الجبِل أوضة بِتْطُلّ عالجبِل
bathroom	*ɦammēm*	حمّام
room with a private bathroom	*ūḍa ma3 ɦammēm*	أوضة مع حمّام
common/shared bathroom	*ɦammēm muštárak*	حمّام مُشْترك
to shower, bathe	*tɦámmam (yitɦámmam)*	تْحمّم (يِتْحمّم)
shower	*[shower]* *ɦammēm*	شاوِر حمّام
bath towel	*mánšafit ɦammēm*	منْشفِة حمّام
shampoo	*[shampoo]*	شامْبو
hair dryer	*[ᶠséchoir]*	سِشْوار
swimming pool	*[ᶠpiscine]*	پيسين
beach	*šaṭṭ (šṭūṭ)*	شطّ (شْطوط)
beach towel	*mánšafit báɦir*	منْشفِة بحِر
sauna	*[ᶠsauna]*	سوْنا
gym	*[gym]*	جيم
massage	*[ᶠmassage]*	مساج
iron	*mikwēyi*	مِكْوايِة
dry cleaning	*[dry clean]*	دْراي كْلين
beverages	*mašrūbēt*	مشْروبات

internet	*[internet]*	إنْترِنْت
tissues	*[Kleenex]*	كْلينيْكْس
safe, lock box	*xázni*	خزْنِة
bed	*táxit (txūt)*	تخِت (تْخوت)
pillow	*mxáddi* *takkēyi*	مْخدِّة تكّايِة
covers, bedspread	*šáršaf (šarāšif)*	شرْشف (شراشِف)
blanket	*ɧrēm*	حْرام
transportation map	*xarīţit ilmuwāşalēt*	خريطِةْ المُواصلات
city map	*xarīţit ilmadīni*	خريطِةْ المدينِة
emergency numbers	*arʔām iţţawāriʔ*	أرْقام الطّوارِئ

Expressions

○

I need an iron.	*3āyiz mikwēyi.*	عايِز مِكْوايِة.
I want to get this suit ironed.	*báddi íkwi háydi -lbádli.*	بدّي إكْوي هَيْدي البدْلِة.
Is there a hair dryer in the room?	*fī šī [ᶠséchoir] bi-lʔūḑa?*	في شي سيشْوار بالأوضة؟
I want to know the location of the closest gym and its schedule.	*báddi á3rif maɧáll áʔrab [gym] w mwa3īdu.*	بدّي أعْرِف محلّ أقْرب جيم ومْواعيدو.

I want to have these laundered/ dry-cleaned.	*báddi íb3at háwdi -ttyēb 3a-lmáṣbaɣa/ 3a-d[dry clean].*	بدّي إبْعت هَوْدي التّياب عالمصْبغة/ عالدّراي كْلينر.
Can you give me a wake-up call at 6 a.m.?	*fīkun twa33ūni -ssē3a sítti iṣṣúbuḥ?*	فيكُن تْوَعّوني السّاعة سِتّة الصُّبُح؟
I have a tour to the south tomorrow morning.	*3índi [tour] 3a-lijnūb búkra -ṣṣúbuḥ.*	عِنْدي تور عالِجْنوب بُكْرا الصُّبُح.
May I have the breakfast to go?	*fíyi ēxud ittirwīʔa [take-away]?*	فِيي آخُد التّرْويقة تايْك أَواي؟
May I have the dinner delivered to my room?	*fíyi ēxud il3áša bi-ūḍti?*	فِيي آخُد العشا بِأوضْتي؟
I want tissues for the room, please.	*báddi [Kleenex] la-lʔūḍa, [please].*	بدّي كْلينيْكْس للأوضة، پْليز.
I don't want my room cleaned today.	*ma báddi ūḍti titnáḍḍaf ilyōm.*	ما بدّي أوضْتي تِتْنضّف اليوْم.
Is tomorrow an official holiday?	*búkra 3íṭli rasmíyyi?*	بُكْرا عِطْلِة رسْمية؟
Will the museum be open?	*bikūn fētiḥ ilmátḥaf?*	بيكون فاتح المتْحف؟

Renting an Apartment أجار شِقّة

Renting a شِقّة *ší??a* **apartment** anywhere is not easy, but being prepared for what to expect always makes things much smoother. Rent in Lebanon is significantly cheaper than in the U.S. or Europe–though, prices have gone up over the years and can vary significantly, depending on where you are looking and the level of amenities you require in the apartment. In Beirut, rent tends to be much more expensive than in the suburbs. Likewise, prices in the northern Christian areas tend to be higher than cities that host fewer expats, such as Tripoli or Tyre. You can rent an apartment through the official channels (rental agencies), informally (through subleasing), through a سِمْسار *simsār* **broker**, or directly from a صاحِب المِلك *ṣāħib ilmílik* **landlord** or صاحْبِة المِلك *ṣāħbit ilmílik* **landlady**. Depending on the apartment building, the rent you're quoted may or may not include utilities, taxes, etc., so it's always better to check what is covered, and what you'll need to pay extra for.

Looking for an Apartment

○ صباحو شباب. قالولي إنّو إنْتو بْتعْرْفوا[1] إذا في بْيوت للأجار هوْن. فيكُن تْساعْدوني؟

◇ أيْه مظْبوط. عم بِتْنبِّش[2] عَ بيْت[3] مفْروش أوْ مِش مفْروش؟

○ مِش مفْروش.[4]

◇ في تْنيْن. واحد بِهيْدي البِنايِة أوضْتيْن[5] نوْم. وواحد بِشِقّة بِآخِر الشّارِع تْلات أُوَض[6] نوْم.

○ أوْكيْ، فاضي هلّق؟ فيك تْفرْجيني الشِّقّة اللي بِهيْدي البِنايِة؟[7]

○ Good morning, gentlemen. I was told you would be the ones to ask about apartments for rent around here. Can you help?

◇ Yep, that would be us. Are you looking for furnished or unfurnished?

○ Unfurnished.

◇ There are two. One is in this building with two bedrooms. The other is down the street and has three bedrooms.

○ Okay. Are you available now? Can you show me the one you have in this building?

○ *ṣabāḫu šabēb. ʔālūli ínnu íntu btá3rfu[1] íza fī byūt la-lʔajār hōn. fīkun tsē3dūni?*

◇ *ē, mazbūṭ. 3am bi-tnábbiš[2] 3a bēt[3] mafrūš aw miš mafrūš?*

○ *miš mafrūš.[4]*

◇ *fī tnēn. wāḫad bi-háydi -lbinēyi ūḍtēn[5] nōm. w wāḫad bi-šíʔʔa bi-ēxir iššēri3 tlēt úwaḍ[6] nōm.*

○ *okē, fāḍi hállaʔ? fīk tfarjīni -ššíʔʔa -lli bi-háydi -lbinēyi?[7]*

[1] (lit. they told me that you would know)

2 = تْفتِّش *tfáttiš*

3 شِقّة *ší??a* **apartment**

[4] = بدون عفِش *bidūn 3áfiš*

[5] = غِرْفْتين *ɣirftēn*

[6] = غِرف *ɣíraf*

[7] = إذا ما عنْدك شي، مُمْكِن تْفرْجيني ياهُن؟ *íza ma 3índak šī, múmkin tfarjīni yēhun?*

2

ASKING ABOUT DETAILS

○ كم أوضة وحمّام فِيا الشِّقّة؟
◇ أوضْتينْ نوْم، أوضِةْ خادْمِة[1]، وحمّامينْ.
○ وبِالآد حاطّين إنّو المطْبخ نافْضينو جْديد؟[2]
◇ أيْه، مظْبوط. لْحقيني.[3]

○ How many bedrooms and bathrooms are there in the apartment?
◇ Two bedrooms, a maid's room, and two bathrooms.
○ And the ad says the kitchen has been renovated?
◇ Yes, that's right. Follow me.

○ *kam ūḍa w ħammēm fíya, -šší??a?*
◇ *ūḍtēn nōm, ūḍit xēdmi*[1], *w ħammēmēn.*
○ *w bi-l?[ad] ħāṭṭīn ínnu -lmáṭbax nāfḍīnu jdīd?*[2]
◇ *ē, maẓbūṭ. lħa?īni.*[3]

[1] = غِرْفِةْ صانْعة *ɣírfit ṣān3a*

[2] = بِالإعْلان كاتْبين إنّو مْجدِّدين المطْبخ؟ *bi-l?i3lēn kētbīn ínnu mjaddidīn ilmáṭbax?*

[3] = صحيح، تعِي معِي. *ṣaħīħ, tá3i má3i.*

3

Asking about rent

○ قدّيْ الأجار لهَيْدي الشِّقّة؟
◇ خمْسْمية دوْلار بِالشّهِر. ما بِتْلاقي شِقّة بِهَيْدا السِّعِر بِهَيْدا الحيّ.
○ بسّ قِلْتِلي إنّو أنا كمان مسْؤولِة عن الكهْربا والميّ وهيْك[1]؟
◇ أيْه، المِسْتأْجِر مسْؤول عنُّن.

○ How much is the monthly rent for this unit?
◇ It's $500 a month. You won't find such a price in this neighborhood.
○ But you said I'm responsible for utilities, too?
◇ Yes, the tenant pays those.

○ *ʔaddē -lʔajār la-háydi -ššíʔʔa?*
◇ *xamsmīt dólar bi-ššáhir. ma bitlēʔi šíʔʔa bi-háyda -ssí3ir bi-háyda -lħayy.*
○ *bass ʔiltíli ínnu ána kamēn masʔūli 3an ilkáhraba w ilmáyy w hēk*[1]*?*
◇ *ē, -lmistájir masʔūl 3ánnun.*

[1] (lit. electricity, water, etc.); = الخدمات *ilxadamēt*

Lebanese youth normally live at home until they're married; as a result, if you're looking for roommates or flatmates, they're more likely to be other expats in the same situation.

Specifying needs

o حبّيْت الشّقّة، بسّ حاسّة إنّو غالْية، خْصوصي إنّو ما في زَوايِد.

◇ شو نوْع الزّوايِد يَلّي عم بِتْنبّْشي[1] عْلَيا مدام؟

o أنا بْروح عالجيم[2] كِلّ يوْم، بِسْتعْمِل الإنْترْنِت، عايْزِة أيْ سي[3].
وهَيْدي الشّقّة ما الهَيْقة فِيا شي مِنُّن وفوْق هَيْدا وكِلّو، غالْيِة.

◇ فينا نْحُطِّلِك أيْ سي[4] عَ حْسابْنا[5]، إذا هَيْدا بيغيرِّلِك رأْيِك.

o I like this apartment, but I feel the price is too high, especially since I get no amenities.

◇ What amenities are you looking for, ma'am?

o Well, I go to the gym every day, I use the internet, I need AC... and this place doesn't seem to have any of these, and most of all, it's expensive.

◇ We can add an AC for you at no additional cost, if that makes a difference.

o *ɧabbēt iššíʔʔa, bass ɧāssi ínnu ɣālyi, xṣūṣi ínnu ma fī zawēyid.*

◇ *šū nō3 izzawēyid yálli 3am bitnábbši[1] 3láya, [Fmadame]?*

o *ána brūɧ 3a-l[gym][2] kill yōm, bistá3mil ilʔ[internet], 3āyzi [AC][3]. w háydi -ššíʔʔa ma -lháyʔa fíya šī mínnun w fōʔ háyda w kíllu, ɣālyi.*

◇ *fīna nɧuṭṭílik [AC][4] 3a ɧsēbna[5], íza háyda biɣayyírlik ráʔyik.*

1 = بِتْفتّْشي *bitfáttši*

2 = عالنّادي *3a-nnēdi*

3 = بدّي مُكيِّف *báddi mukáyyif*

4 = نْركّبْلِك مُكيِّف *nrakkíblik mukáyyif*

5 = عَ نفقِتْنا *3a nafaʔítna*

ASKING ABOUT UTILITIES

- ○ هَيْدي الشِّقّة فِيا عدّاد ميّ وكهْربا؟
- ◇ أيْه دْموازيْل. وَلا يْهِمِّك.[1] كِلّ بْيِنْعدّ عالقدّ.
- ○ أوْكي، وذكِّرْني، في أيْ سي وشوْفاج سانْترال[2] بِالشِّقّة؟
- ◇ لأ، بسّ حاطّين أيْ سي بِكِلّ الأُوَض. في سِخِن وبارِد.
- ○ كْتير مْنيح.[3] وفي موْتوْر؟ لِأنّو سْمِعِت إنّو لازِم يْكون عِنْدي اِشْتِراك لأِنّو الكهْربا كْتير بْتِنْقطع بِلِبْنان.
- ◇ أيْه أكيد.[4] الكهْربا هوْن ما إلا وَقِت، لهيْك الشِّقّة والبِنايِة كِلّا مَوْصولِة عالموْتوْر. بْيِدور وَحْدو[5] بسّ تْروح الكهْربا. ما في كم ثانْيِة.

- ○ Does the apartment have meters for water and electricity?
- ◇ Yes, miss. Not to worry. Everything is tracked accurately.
- ○ Okay, and remind me, was there a central heating system in the unit?
- ◇ No, but we put air-conditioners in all units, which you can set on hot or cold.
- ○ Great. What about generator service? I heard I'll need it because the power goes out a lot here.
- ◇ Yes, absolutely. Since electricity is unpredictable in Lebanon, the apartment and the whole building are hooked up to a generator service, which turns on automatically when the power goes out. There's a few seconds' gap.

- ○ *háydi -šší??a fíya 3addēd mayy w káhraba?*
- ◇ *ē, [[F]demoiselle]. wála yhímmik.[1] kill byin3ádd 3a-l?ádd.*
- ○ *okē, w zakkírni, fī [AC] w [[F]chauffage central][2] bi-šší??a?*
- ◇ *la?, bass ḥāṭṭīn [AC] bi-kíll il?úwaḍ. fī síxin w bērid.*
- ○ *ktīr mnīḥ.[3] w fī [[F]moteur]? li-ánnu smí3it ínnu lēzim ykūn 3índi ištirāk li-ánnu -lkáhraba ktīr btin?áṭa3 bi-libnēn.*

◇ ē, akīd.[4] -lkáhraba hōn ma íla wáʔit, la-hēk iššíʔʔa w ilbinēyi kílla mawṣūli 3a-l[Fmoteur]. bidūr wáɧdu[5] bass trūɧ ilkáhraba. ma fī kam sēnyi.

[1] = ما تِعْتلي همّ. ma tí3tali hamm.

[2] = مْكيِّف وتِسْخين مركزي mukáyyif w tisxīn márkazi

[3] = تمام tamēm

[4] = أيْ طبْعاً ē, ṭáb3an

[5] = بيدور أوْتوْماتيك bidūr [Fautomatique]

الكهْربا -lkáhraba **power/electricity** in Lebanon is not available 24/7 and بْتِنْقطع btinʔáṭa3 **goes out** every few hours. However, virtually all apartment buildings have a generator service, referred to by its French name, موْتور *[Fmoteur],* that kicks on within seconds of the power going out. However, the generator will stop if you draw more electricity than your amperage allows. People say تكّ الدّيجوْنْكْتور *takk id[Fdisjoncteur]* or فقس الدّيجوْنْكْتور *fáʔas id[Fdisjoncteur]* **The circuit breaker has tripped**. It's a good term to know, as this happens quite often in apartments with insufficient amperage for the household usage.

6

Signing the contract

○ فينا نمْضي الكوْنْترا[1] بُكْرا فإذاً؟

◇ أيْه، إذا الله راد. بسّ بدّك تِدْفع شهْريْن ديپوْسِت، وشهِر مْقدّم.

○ أوْكيْ، رح إبْعتْلِك صورة عن الپاسْپوْر فإذاً.

◇ أوْكيْ، ما في مشْكل. ومْنِمْضي كمان ليسْتا عْلَيا كِلّ الغْراض اللي بِالشِّقّة[2].

○ Shall we sign the contract tomorrow then?

◇ Yes, God willing, but there will be a two-month deposit and one month paid in advance.

○ Okay, I'll send you a copy of my passport then.

◇ No problem. And we will also sign a list of the items included in the apartment.

○ *fīna nímḍi -l[contrat][1] búkra fa-ízan?*

◇ *ē, íza álla rād. bass báddak tídfa3 šahrēn [deposit], w šáhir mʔáddam.*

○ *okē, raḫ ib3átlik ṣūra 3an ilpaspōr fa-ízan.*

◇ *okē, ma fī máškal. w mnímḍi kamēn līsta 3láya kill liɣrāḍ -lli bi-ššíʔʔa[2].*

[1] = العقِد *-l3áʔid*

[2] = مُحْتويات الشِّقة *muḫtūyēt iššíʔʔa*

Extended Dialoguen

○ كم مِترْ الشِّقّة؟[1]

◇ تْلات ميةْ مِترْ مْربّع.

○ تْلات أُوَض[2] نوم. ما هيْك؟

◇ أيْه، تْفضّلي تْفرْجي بِعَيْنَيْكي. أحْلى شِقّة عم نْفرْجِيا هَيْدا الشّهِر.[3]

○ فيك تْخبرّْني شْوَيّ أكْتر[4] عن الأدَوات الكهْربائية؟

◇ كِلُّن سْتانْلِس سْتيل. وجْداد[5]. إنْتي بِتْكوني أوّل حدا بْيِسْتعْمِلُن.

○ أوْكي، وفي أيْ سي وشوْفاج مركزي؟

◇ أيْه، هَوْدي كمان بعْدْنا حاطّينُن جْديد، فأكيد ما رح تْواجْهي مشاكِل معُن.

○ والحيّ؟ آمِن؟[6]

◇ مِن أأمن الأحْياء بِالبلد! مِن هيْك الأجار يمْكِن أغْلى شْوَيّ مْن الأسْعار اللي عم بِتْشوفِين.

○ عالأكيد أغْلى. بسّ جَوْزي كْتير حبّو[7]، وكان بدّو ياني شوفو. وبِفْتِكِر أنا كمان حبّيْتو.

◇ تمام! بْتْحِبّي إتْناقَش بِبْنود الأجار مع جَوْزِك أَوْ معِك؟

○ بِرْجع بُكْرا الصُّبِح مع مايْك، ومْنِمْضي كِلّ شي ساعِتا، إذا فيك؟ شو بدّك وْراق مِنّا؟

◇ باسْپوْراتْكُن تْنَيْناتْكُن. ورِسالِة مِن قِسِم شْؤون المْوَظّفين مِن شِرْكاتْكُن تْنَيْناتْكُن كبرْهان إنّو عِنْدْكُن وَظيفِة هوْن. بْتعْرْفي، لِأنّو منْكُن لِبْنانِيّين، مجْبورين نْقدِّم هالِوْراق لصاحِب المُلْك. ومْنُطْلُب كمان ديپوْسِت شهْريْن أجار.

○ أيْه، ما في مشْكل. ومايْك جاب الوَرْقة مِن شِرْكْتو. وأنا بِشْتِغِل عَ حْسابي، فبِقْدر جِبْلك رُخْصِة الشِّرْكة.

◇ عظيم! بدُّكُن العقِد بِالإنْجْليزي؟

○ بِفْتِكِر أظْبط أيْه إذا بِالإنْجْليزي، هيْك مِنْطمِّن بالْنا.[8]

◇ تمام. بْجيبِلْكُن العقِد بِالإنْجْليزي.

○ كْتير مْنيح. طيِّب، أنا ومايْك مِنْشوفك بُكْرا. عالتِّسْعة مْنيح؟[9]

◇ إن الله راد. بْشوفْكُن بُكْرا.

○ Well, how many square meters is this apartment?

◇ 300 square meters.

○ Three bedrooms, right?

◇ Yes, go ahead and have a look for yourself. It's the best unit we're managing this month.

○ Can you tell me more about the appliances?

◇ All the appliances are stainless steel, brand new. You would be the first tenant to live here since we installed them.

○ Okay, and is there AC and central heating?

◇ Yes, those have also been installed recently, so you shouldn't have any problems with them.

○ What about the neighborhood? Is it safe?

◇ One of the safest in the country, ma'am. That's why rent is probably a bit higher than other quotes you've been getting.

○ That it is, but my husband really liked it, so he wanted me to come see it for myself, and I think I do, too.

◇ Great! Shall I discuss the rental terms with your husband or with you?

○ I'll come back with Mike tomorrow morning if that's okay, and we can sign everything then? What documents do you need from us?

◇ Both of your passports, and a letter from both your companies that proves that you have jobs here. You know, because you're not citizens, we're required to present that documentation to the landlord. And we'll need a two-month deposit.

o Yes, no problem. Mike has already gotten his, and I have my own business, so I can just bring you the business license.

◇ Great! Will you need the contract in English?

o That would be best if it's in English. It will put our minds at ease.

◇ Wonderful. I'll bring the English version.

o Excellent. Well, Mike and I will see you tomorrow. Shall we say 9:00am?

◇ God willing. See you then.

o *kam mitr iššíʔʔa?*[1]

◇ *tlēt mīt mitr mrábba3.*

o *tlēt úwaḍ*[2] *nōm. ma hēk?*

◇ *ē, tfáḍḍali tfárrji bi-3aynáyki. áɦla šíʔʔa 3am nfarrjíya háyda -ššáhir.*[3]

o *fīk txabbírni šwayy áktar*[4] *3an ilʔadawēt ilkahrabēʔíyyi?*

◇ *kíllun [stainless steal]. w jdēd*[5]*. ínti bitkūni áwwal ɦáda byistá3milun.*

o *okē, w fī [AC] w [*[F]*chauffage] márkazi?*

◇ *ē, háwdi kamēn bá3dna ɦāṭṭīnun jdīd, fa-akīd ma raɦ twējhi mašēkil má3un.*

o *w ilɦáyy? ēmin?*[6]

◇ *min áʔman ilʔaɦyēʔ bi-lbálad! min hēk ilʔajār yímkin áɣla šwayy mn ilʔas3ār -lli 3am bitšūfiyun.*

o *3a-lʔakīd áɣla. bass jáwzi ktīr ɦábbu*[7]*, w kēn báddu yēni šūfu. w bíftikir ána kamēn ɦabbáytu.*

◇ *tamēm! bitɦíbbi itnēʔaš bi-bunūd ilʔajār ma3 jáwzik aw má3ik?*

o *bírja3 búkra -ṣṣúbuɦ ma3 [Mike], w mnímḍi kill šī sē3íta, íza fīk? šū báddak wrāʔ mínna?*

◇ *paspōrātkun tnaynētkun. w risēli min ʔísim šʔūn ilmwaẓẓafīn min širkētkun tnaynētkun ka-burhān ínnu 3índkun waẓīfi hōn. btá3rfi, li-ánnu mánnkun libnēniyyīn, majbūrīn nʔáddim ha-liwrāʔ la-ṣāɦib ilmílik. w mnúṭlub kamēn [deposit] šahrēn ajār.*

o *ē, ma fī máškal. w [Mike] jēb ilwárʔa min šírktu. w ána bištíɣil 3a ɦsēbi, fa-bíʔdar jíblak rúxṣit iššírki.*

◇ *3aẓīm! báddkun il3áʔid bi-lʔinglīzi?*

o *bíftikir áẓbaṭ ē, íza bi-lʔinglīzi, hēk minṭámmin bēlna.*[8]

◇ *tamēm. bjībílkun il3áʔid bi-lʔinglīzi.*

○ *ktīr mnīɧ. ţáyyib, ána w [Mike] minšūfak búkra. 3a-ttís3a mnīɧ?*[9]
◇ *in álla rād. bšūfkun búkra.*

[1] = قدّيْ مساحِةْ الشِّقّة؟ *ʔaddē masēɧit iššíʔʔa?*

[2] = غِرف *ɣíraf*

[3] = خِدي برْمِة، أحْلى شِقّة معْروضة. *xídi bármi, áɧla šíʔʔa ma3rūɖa.* **Take a look around. It's the nicest apartment available.**

[4] = فيك تعْطيني فِكْرة *fīk ta3ţīni fíkra* **can you give me an idea...**

[5] = كِلُّن بِلْنايْلون *kíllun bi-n[nylon]* (lit. they're all nylon) means they're brand new.

[6] الحيّ رايِق؟ *-lɧayy rāyiʔ?* **Is it a quiet neighborhood?**

[7] = كْتير عجبو *ktīr 3ájabu*

[8] ما بْتِفْرُق. *ma btífruʔ.* **It doesn't matter.**

[9] = تمام. برْكي مْنِلْتقى بُكْرا عاتِّسْعة؟ *tamēm. bárki mníltaʔi búkra 3a-ttís3a?*

Vocabulary

apartment	*šíʔʔa (šíʔaʔ)*	شِقّة (شِقق)
(bed)room	*ūḑa (úwaḑ)*	أوضة (أُوَض)
two rooms	*ūḑtēn*	أوضْتينْ
three rooms	*tlēt úwaḑ*	تْلات أُوَض
floor, story	*ţābiʔ*	طابِق
apartment building	*mábna sákani*	مبْنى سكني
doorman	*buwwēb* *nāţūr*	بُوّاب ناطور
housekeeping	*farīʔ ittandīf*	فريق التّنْضيف
to rent	*ájjar (yʔájjir)*	أجّر (يْأجِّر)
rent	*ajār*	أجار
real estate agent, rental agent	*simsār*	سِمْسار
brokerage fees	*sámsara*	سمْسرة
owner, landlord	*şāɧib*	صاحِب
contract	*3áʔid (3ʔūd)*	عقِد (عْقود)
furnished	*mafrūš*	مفْروش
non-furnished	*miš mafrūš*	مِش مفْروش
kitchen	*máţbax (maţābix)*	مطْبخ (مطابِخ)
bathroom	*ɧammēm*	حمّام
balcony	*[Fbalcon]* *baránda*	بلْكوْن برنْدا

stairs	*dáraj*	درج
(utility) meter	*3addēd*	عدّاد
electricity	*káhraba*	كهْربا
water	*mayy*	ميّ
(natural) gas	*ɣāz*	غاز
telephone	*[Ftéléphone]*	تِلفوْن
internet	*[internet]*	إنْترِنْت
washing machine	*ɣassēli*	غسّالِة
stove	*máwʔad*	مَوْقد
refrigerator	*tallēji*	تلّاجِة
heater	*daffēyi*	دفّايِة
light shaft, skylight	*mánwar*	منْوَر
security deposit	*taʔmīn*	تأْمين
(itemized) list	*lēyħa* *līsta*	لايْحة ليسْتة

Expressions

Can I rent the apartment by the day?	*fíyi istáʔjir iššíʔʔa bi-linhār/nahāri?*	فِيي إسْتأْجِر الشِّقّة بِالنِْهار/نهاري؟
We only need/want the apartment for two months.	*bass 3āyzīn/ báddna -ššíʔʔa šahrēn.*	بسّ عايزين/بدّْنا الشِّقّة شهْريْن.

Can I put a screen on this window?	*fíyi ḫuṭṭ šrīṭ 3a háyda -ššibbēk?*	فِيي حُطّ شْريط عَ هَيْدا الشِّبّاك؟
Can I paint the walls?	*fíyi ídhan ilḫīṭān?*	فِيي إدْهن الحيطان؟
Do you know a cleaning lady who can come clean the apartment once a week?	*btá3rif šī mára fíya tíji tnáḍḍif iššíʔʔa márra bi-ljím3a?*	بْتعْرِف شي مرا فِيا تِجي تْنضِّف الشِّقّة مرّة بِالجِمْعة؟
Is there a gardener who can take care of the plants?	*fī šī jnaynēti fī yihtámm bi-ššatlēt?*	في شي جْنَيْناتي في[1] يِهْتمّ بِالشّتْلات؟

[1] في *fī* appears twice in this sentence. The first is the more common **there is/are**, while the second is a variant form of فِيو *fíyu* **he can**.

◇

You have received the apartment with these items included, and you have to return it in the same condition you received it in.	*stálamit iššíʔʔa w fíya ha-liɣrāḍ, w lēzim tírja3 tsállima mítil ma kēnit.*	سْتلِمت الشِّقّة وفِيا هالغْراض، ولازِم ترْجع تْسلِّما مِتِل ما كانِت.
If you would like to change anything, that's fine, but you have to return it as it was before you move out.	*íza ḫābib tɣayyír šī, ma fī máškal, bass lēzim tridd kill šī mítil ma kēn ʔábil ma tfill.*	إذا حابِب تْغيرّ شي، ما في مشْكل، بسّ لازِم تْردّ كِلّ شي مِتِل ما كان قبِل ما تْفِلّ.
You can change the door's lock, but put back the old one before moving out.	*fīk tɣáyyir ʔífl ilbēb, bass ridd ilʔífl ilʔadīm ʔábil ma tfill.*	فيك تْغيرِّ قِفْل الباب، بسّ رِدّ القِفْل القديم قبِل ما تْفِلّ.

You should give the doorman a finder's fee for telling you about the apartment.	*lēzim tá3ţi -nnāţūr šū ma byíţla3 min xāţrak li-ánnu ʔállak 3an iššíʔʔa.*	لازِم تعْطي النّاطور شو ما بْيِطْلع مِن خاطْرك لِأنّو قالّك عن الشِّقّة.
Brokerage fees are usually a month's rent, but they could just be half a month.	*-ssámsara ijmēlan šáhir ajār, bass fíya tkūn nuşş šáhir.*	السّمْسرة إجْمالاً شهِر أجار، بسّ فيا تْكون نُصّ شهِر.
There's a cleaning lady that many tenants in this building speak very highly off. I'll give you her number.	*fī sitt bitnáḍḍif la-káza mistáʔjir bi-lbinēyi w byíђku ktīr mnīђ fíya. ba3ţīk ráʔma íza bitђíbb.*	في سِتّ بِتْنضِّف لكذا مِسْتأْجِر بِالبِنايِة وبْيِحْكوا كْتير مْنيح فِيا. بعْطيك رقْما إذا بِتْحِبّ.

Dealing with a Housekeeper

حكي مع الخادْمِة

Except for families with old money, rarely would you see in Lebanon households that employ Lebanese housekeepers. Most hire housekeepers from Southeast Asia and Africa. There are at least three ways to hire a housekeeper. The first is longterm, through a maid agency, where the household pays a yearly amount to cover the paperwork for the maid and to fly her to Lebanon, as well as a monthly fee. The second is 'as needed,' by going through agencies–and these are normally different agencies than those that bring long-term housekeepers to Lebanon.) These 'as needed' agencies typically bring over several maids and find work for them in different households, paying them by the hour, rather than employing them fulltime in one household. You can also get an 'as needed' housekeeper directly by hiring her directly if she already live in Lebanon. This is the riskiest option, however, as most such housekeepers are undocumented and in Lebanon illegally. She might have run away from her original employers' home or overstayed her visa. And while these independent housekeepers charge less per, you may get in trouble for hiring illegally.

Confirming with the Housekeeper

○ هاي ميا، كيفِك؟ معِك ندى.
◇ اه هاي دْمْوازيْل ندى.
○ بعْدْنا عَ مَوْعدْنا الخميس؟ البيْت كِلّو؟[1]
◇ أيْه دْمْوازيْل. بْشوفِك الخميس.

○ Hello, Mia, how are you? This is Nada.
◇ Oh, hello, Miss Nada!
○ Are we still on for Thursday, for the whole house?
◇ Yes, miss. I'll see you on Thursday.

○ *[hi] [Mia], kīfik? má3ik náda.*
◇ *āh [hi], [F demoiselle] náda.*
○ *bá3dna 3a máw3adna -lxamīs? -lbēt kíllu?*[1]
◇ *ē, [F demoiselle]. bšūfik ilxamīs.*

[1] رح تِجي الخميس متِل ما تّفقْنا تْنضّفيلي البيْت كِلّو؟ *raђ tíji -lxamīs mítil ma ttafáʔna tnaḍḍfīli -lbēt kíllu?* **Are you coming on Thursday, as we agreed, to clean the whole house for me?**

Housekeeper is خادْمِة *xádmi* (lit. servant) or صانْعة *ṣān3a* (lit. maker) in Levantine Arabic. Although common, both terms are somewhat derogatory, so some people opt to say اللي بِتْنضّفْلي *-lli bitnaḍḍífli* (lit. one who cleans for me), which has a somewhat better connotation than the other terms.

2

Rescheduling

o هاي دْمْوازيْل دانا. معِك[1] مارِيا.

◇ اه هاي مارِيا. إنْتي مْنيحة؟ بعْدْنا عَ مَوْعدْنا بُكْرا؟

o مِن هيْك عم دِقّ ميس. منّي مْنيحة.[2] فينا نْأجِّل؟

◇ أكيد! أَيْ متى بْتِفْتِكْري رح فيكي تِجي؟

o مرْسي ميس. الأرْجح الجِمْعة. هيْك بعْطي حالي يَوْمينْ تَصير أحْسن.

◇ أوْكيْ، أيْه، أكيد. فِيي أنا إمْرُق آخْدِك الجِمْعة.

◇ Hello, Miss Dana. This is Maria.

o Oh, hi, Maria. Are you okay? Are we still on for tomorrow?

◇ That's why I'm calling, ma'am. I'm not feeling too well. Can we reschedule?

o Sure. When do you think you'll be able to come?

◇ Thanks, miss. Probably Friday. It will give me a couple days to get better.

o Okay, yes, sure. I can come get you on Friday.

o *[hi], [Fdemoiselle] dāna. má3ik[1] [Maria].*

◇ *āh [hi] [Maria]. ínti mnīħa? bá3dna 3a máw3adna búkra?*

o *min hēk 3am diʔʔ [miss]. mánni mnīħa.[2] fīna nʔájjil?*

◇ *akīd! áymata btíftikri raħ fīki tíji?*

o *[Fmerci] [miss]. -lʔárjaħ iljím3a. hēk bá3ṭi ħāli yawmēn ta-ṣīr áħsan.*

◇ *okē, ē, akīd. fíyi ána ímruʔ ēxdik ljím3a.*

[1] (lit. with you) This is the standard expression to indentify yourself on the phone. To ask who is calling: مين معي؟ *mīn má3i?* (lit. Who is [talking] with me?)

[2] عم إتِّصِل فيكي لخبرِّك إنّو مِش رح إقْدر إجي لعِنْدِك بُكرا. *3am ittíṣil fīki la-xábbrik ínnu miš raħ íʔdar íji la-3índik búkra.* **I'm calling to let you know that I'm won't be able to come to your place tomorrow.**

③

Answering questions

o مادام، أيّا ممْسحة فِيي إسْتعْمِل؟
◇ يَلّي حدّ الباب نْضيفة وجْديدِة.
o أوْكي، تمام، مرْسي.
◇ مرْسي إلِك!

◇ Ma'am, which mop can I use?
o The one by the door is new and clean!
◇ Okay, great. Thanks!
o Thank *you!*

o *[Fmadame], áyya mámsaɧa fíyi istá3mil?*
◇ *yálli ɧadd ilbēb nḍīfi w jdīdi.*
o *okē, tamēm, [Fmerci].*
◇ *[Fmerci] ílik!*

While it's most definitely not an issue in every household, human rights violations of housekeepers have been a huge problem in Lebanon. These include starving housekeepers, not allowing them to contact their families, not allowing them their days off, etc. Because these housekeepers make a lot more in Lebanon than they would back in their home countries, many end up just putting up with the circumstances for the length of their contract, so that they can send money back home to their families. Civil society has been actively involved in the issue, however, and are empowering and giving these women (and occasionally men) a voice to fight for their rights.

GIVING THE HOUSEKEEPER A RIDE

◇ هاي مادام، معِك لينْدا.
○ هاي لينْدا، بِكي شي؟[1] فِيي دِقِّلِك بعْد شْوَيّ؟
◇ أيْه مادام. سوْري. بسّ يَلّي كانوا بدُّن يْوَصّْلوني لعِنْدِك ما رح فِيُنْ يْجيبوني بقى. كان بدّي شوف إذا فيكي تِجي إنْتي تاخْديني.[2]
○ أيْه فِيي، بسّ مْأخّرة شي عشْر دْقايِق.[3]

◇ Hi, ma'am, this is Linda.
○ Hi Linda, are you okay? Can I call you in a bit?
◇ Yes, yes, ma'am. I'm sorry. It's just that my ride fell through. And I was wondering if you could pick me up.
○ Yes, I can, but I'll be about 10 minutes late.

◇ *[hi] [Fmadame], má3ik [Linda].*
○ *[hi] [Linda], bíki šī?*[1] *fíyi diʔʔílik ba3d šwayy?*
◇ *ē, [Fmadame]. [sorry]. bass yálli kēnu báddun ywaṣṣlūni la-3índik ma raḫ fíyun yjībūni báʔa. kēn báddi šūf íza fīki tíji ínti tēxdīni.*[2]
○ *ē, fíyi, bass mʔáxxara šī 3ašr dʔāyiʔ.*[3]

[1] في شي ضروري؟ *fī šī ḍarūri?* **Is there something urgent?**

[2] فيكي تمِرْقي وَرايي؟ *fīki timírʔi warāyi?* **Can you pick me up?** (lit. pass behind me)

[3] لأ صعّبِة. بسّ فِيِّ إبْعتْلِك أوبر. *laʔ, ṣáb3i. bass fíyi ib3átlik [Uber].* **No, that'd be hard [for me]. But I can send an Uber for you.**

5

Specifying tasks (1)

○ تانْيا، بعْرِف قِلْتِلِك إنّو مْنعْمِل البيْت كِلّو اليوْم، بسّ لازِم فِلّ لِأنّو عِنْدي شي.[1] خلّينا نعْمِل المطْبخ والأُوَض بسّ.

◇ أكيد دْمْوازيْل، مِتِل ما بدِّك.

○ عظيم. مرْسي. وفِيي وَصّلِك ع طريقي.

◇ ييه بْكون ممْنونْتِك دْمْوازيْل.

○ Tania, I know I told you that we'd do the whole house today, but I have a thing I have to go to. Let's only do the kitchen and the bedrooms.

◇ Sure, miss. Whatever you want!

○ Excellent. Thank you. And I can give you a ride on my way.

◇ Oh, that would be amazing, miss.

○ *[Tanya], bá3rif ʔiltílik ínnu mná3mil ilbēt kíllu -lyōm, bass lēzim fill li-ánnu 3índi šī.*[1] *xallīna ná3mil ilmáṭbax w ilʔúwaḍ bass.*

◇ *akīd, [F demoiselle], mítil ma báddik.*

○ *3aẓīm. [F merci]. w fíyi wáṣṣlik 3a ṭarīʔi.*

◇ *yī! bkūn mamnūntik, [F demoiselle].*

[1] ما تعْمْلي البيْت كِلّو اليوْم، ما بِتْلحْقي لِأنّي طالْعة. **Don't do the whole house today. You won't have time because I'm going out.**

6

Specifying tasks (2)

o هاي[1] مارِيا، اِلْنا كذا يوْم ما عِنّا ميّ. بقى خلّينا اليوْم بسّ نعْمِل هوفر ونْشيل الغبْرة.

◇ أكيد مدام. عِنْدِك شي تْياب بدُّن كَوْي؟

o اه هَيْدي فِكْرة مْنيحة. أيْه پْليز.

◇ أوْكيْ، رح أعْمِلُن. شي تاني؟

o لأ مرْسي مارِيا. هَوْدي بيكفّوا لليوْم.

◇ أوْكيْ دُمْوازيْل.

o Hey Marla, we haven't had water for days, so let's only vacuum and dust today.

◇ Sure, ma'am. Do you have any clothes I can iron?

o Oh, that's a good idea. Yes, please.

◇ Okay, I'll do that. Anything else?

o No, that's okay, Maria. That would be enough for today.

◇ Okay, miss.

o *[hi][1], [Maria], ílna káza yōm ma 3ínna mayy. báʔa xallīna -lyōm bass ná3mil [hoover] w nšīl ilɣábra.*

◇ *akīd, [Fmadame]. 3índik šī tyēb báddun káwi?*

o *āh háydi fíkra mnīḫa. ē, [please].*

◇ *okē, raḫ ú3milun. šī tēni?*

o *laʔ [Fmerci], [Maria]. háwdi bikáffu la-lyōm.*

◇ *okē, [Fdemoiselle].*

[1] = مرْحبا *máḫaba*

◇ هاي دُمْوازيْل، كيفِك اليوْم؟

○ بْصير أحْسن بسّ البيْت يِنْضف! صرْلي كذا جِمْعة مْسافْرة، مِن هيْك ما دقّيْتِلِك.[1]

◇ اه أيْه قِلْتيلي مرّةْ الماضْيِة دُمْوازيْل.[2]

○ مظْبوط، شِفْتي؟ صرْلا زمان القُصّة.[3]

◇ بِشو لازِم بلِّش؟

○ بعْدْني عم شيل غْراضي مْن الشِّنط بِأوضْتي، فَيِمْكِن أحْسن تْبلِّشي بِالمطْبخ، وبعْدين أوضِةْ السّهْرة[4]، والحمّامات وآخِر شي أوضْتي.

◇ أوْكيْ، تمام. رح بلِّش.

(after the cleaning is done)

◇ كِلّو خُلِص دُمْوازيْل. بْتِحِبّي أعْمِل شي تاني؟

○ لأ، مرْسي، پيا. كِلّو بيجنِّن. يِسْلمو إيديْكي.

◇ مرْسي دُمْوازيْل.

○ تْفضّلي. مرْسي عن جْديد.

◇ دُمْوازيْل، كْتير هالقدّ، مرْسي كْتير.

○ عيْب[5] پيا، وَلَوْ[6]. ما حدا بْيِهْتمّ بِالبيْت مِتِل ما إنْتي بْتِهْتمّي فيه. بقى مرْسي.[7]

◇ أكيد دُمْوازيْل. هَيْدا شِغْلي.

○ قدّ ما كان[8]، مرْسي.

◇ مرْسي إلِك!

◇ Hello, miss. How are you today?

○ Oh, I'll be better when the house is clean! I've been traveling for a few weeks, that's why I hadn't called you.

◇ Oh yeah, you told me last time, miss.

○ Right, see? It's been a while!

◇ What shall I start with?

○ I'm still unpacking my stuff in my bedroom, so it's probably best that you start with the kitchen, then the living room, then the bathrooms, then, finally, my bedroom.

◇ Okay, perfect. I'll get started.

(after the cleaning is done)

◇ All done, miss. Would you like anything else?

○ No, thank you, Pia. It looks great. Bless your hands.

◇ Thank you, miss!

○ Here you go. Thank you again.

◇ Miss, this is so generous. Thank you so much.

○ Don't mention it, Pia. Nobody takes care of the house the way you do. So, thank you!

◇ It's my pleasure, miss. This is my job.

○ Well, still. Thank you.

◇ Thank *you!*

◇ *[hi], [[F]demoiselle], kīfik ilyōm?*

○ *bṣīr áɧsan bass ilbēt yínḍaf! ṣárli káza jím3a msēfra, min hēk ma daʔʔaytílik.*[1]

◇ *āh ē, ʔiltīli marrt ilmāḍyi, [[F]demoiselle].*[2]

○ *mazbūṭ, šífti? ṣárla zamēn ilʔúṣṣa.*[3]

◇ *bi-šū lēzim bálliš?*

○ *bá3dni 3am šīl ɣrāḍi mn iššínaṭ bi-ūḍti, fa-yímkin áɧsan tbállši bi-lmáṭbax, w ba3dēn ūḍit issáhra*[4]*, w ilɧammēmēt w ēxir šī ūḍti.*

◇ *okē, tamēm. raɧ bálliš.*

(after the cleaning is done)

◇ *kíllu xúliṣ, [[F]demoiselle]. bitɧíbbi á3mil šī tēni?*

○ *laʔ, [[F]merci], [Pia]. kíllu bijánnin. yíslamu idáyki.*

◇ *[[F]merci], [[F]demoiselle].*

○ *tfáḍḍali. [[F]merci] 3an jdīd.*

◇ *[[F]demoiselle], ktīr ha-lʔádd, [[F]merci] ktīr.*

○ *3ēb*[5] *[Pia], waláw*[6]*. ma ɧáda byihtámm bi-lbēt mítil ma ínti btihtámmi fī. báʔa [[F]merci].*

◇ *akīd, [ᶠdemoiselle]. háyda šíɣli.*
○ *ʔadd ma kēn*[7], *[ᶠmerci].*
◇ *[ᶠmerci] ílik!*

1 البيْت كْتير وِسِخ بِغْيابْنا، بدّو تنْضِيف ضروري. *-lbēt ktīr wísix bi-ɣyēbna, báddu tanḑīf ḑarūri.* **The house has gotten dirty in our absence and needs cleaning urgently.**

2 = أيْ مظْبوط، خبرّتيني هَيْداك المرّة. *ē, maẓbūţ, xabbartīni haydēk ilmárra.*

3 = أيْ قديمِة الشّغْلِة. *ē, ʔadīmi -ššáɣli.*

4 = أوضِةْ القعْدِة *ūḑit ilʔá3di*

5 عيْب *3ēb* (See note 4 on p. 167)

6 وَلَوْ *waláw* **come on!, please!; you're welcome!**

7 شُكراً يعْطيكي العافْيِة. ريحِةْ نضافِة! *šúkran, ya3ţīki -l3āfyi. rīħit naḑāfi!*

8 (lit. as much as it was) **even so, all the same**

Vocabulary

apartment building	*mábna sákani (mabēni sakaníyyi)*	مبْنى سكني (مباني سكنية)
apartment	*šíʔʔa (šíʔaʔ)*	شِقّة (شِقق)
floor, story	*ţābiʔ (ţawābiʔ)*	طابِق (طَوابِق)
entrance, entry way	*mádxal*	مدْخل
stairs	*dáraj*	درج
gate	*buwwēbi*	بْوّابِة
intercom	*[ᶠinterphone]*	إنْترْفوْن
elevator	*[ᶠascenseur]*	أسانْسور
garbage	*zbēli*	زْبالِة
garage	*[ᶠgarage]*	جراج
doorman	*nāţūr*	ناطور
electricity	*káhraba*	كهْربا
water	*mayy*	ميّ
gas	*ɣāz*	غاز
per hour	*bi-ssē3a*	بِالسّاعة
cleaning	*tanđīf*	تنْضيف
once a week	*márra bi-ljím3a/ bi-lʔusbū3*	مرّة بِالجِمْعة/ بِالأُسْبوع
groceries	*ɣrāđ la-lbēt*	غْراض للبيْت
vegetables	*xúđra*	خُضْرا

fruit(s)	*fwēki*	فْواكِه
(plastic) bag	*kīs (kyēs)*	كيس (كْياس)
luggage, bag	*šánṭa (šínaṭ)*	شنْطة (شِنط)
security	*ámin, [security]*	أمِن، سِكْيوريتي
camera	*[camera]*	كاميرا
roof	*sáṭiḥ (sṭūḥ)*	سطِح (سْطُوح)
basement	*[ᶠdépôt], mistáwda3*	ديپوْ، مِسْتَوْدع
light shaft, skylight	*mánwar*	منْوَر
every other week	*jím3a ē jím3a laʔ*	جِمْعة أيْه جِمْعة لأ
housekeeper, cleaning lady	*ṣān3a* *xādmi* *laffēyi* *-lmára/-ssitt -lli bitnaḍḍífli*	صانْعة خادْمِة لفّايِة المرا/السِّتّ اللي بِتْنضِّفْلي
to fold laundry	*ṭáwa (yíṭwi) -lɣasīl*	طَوى (يِطْوي) الغسيل
to do laundry	*ɣásal (yíɣsil)*	غسل (يِغْسِل)
to iron	*káwa (yíkwi)*	كَوى (يِكْوي)
to collect the laundry (from the clothes line)	*lamm (ylimm) ilɣasīl*	لمّ (يْلِمّ) الغسيل
storage closet	*máxzan*	مخْزن
once a month	*márra bi-ššáhir*	مرّة بِالشّهِر
twice a month	*marrtēn bi-ššáhir*	مرّتيْن بِالشّهِر

Could you please clean the whole house?	*fīki [please] tnáḍḍfi kill ilbēt?*	فيكي پْليز تْنضّفي كِلّ البيْت؟
Could you please just do the bedrooms today?	*fīki [please] bass tá3mli -lʔúwaḍ ilyōm?*	فيكي پْليز بسّ تعْمْلي الأُوَض اليوْم؟
Press on the intercom before you come up.	*díʔʔi 3a-lʔ[ᶠinterphone] ʔábil ma tíṭla3i.*	دِقّي عالإنْترْفوْن قبِل ما تِطْلعي.
Please be mindful as you use water today, we haven't had water in days.	*[please] ntíbhi ínti w 3am tistá3mli -lmayy ilyōm. ṣárlna káza yōm ma 3ínna mayy.*	پْليز انْتبِهي إنْتي وعم تِسْتعْمْلي الميّ اليوْم. صرْلْنا كذا يوْم ما عِنّا ميّ.
The power is out today, so let's not vacuum or iron today. The generator wouldn't be able to handle it. Let's just sweep and mop.	*-lkáhraba maʔṭū3a ilyōm, fa-bála [hoover] aw káwi -lyōm. il[ᶠmoteur] ma byíħmul. xallīna bass nkánnis w nímsaħ.*	الكهربا مقْطوعة اليوْم، فبلا هوفر أَوْ كَوي اليوْم. الموْتور ما بْيحْمُل. خلّينا بسّ نْكنِّس ونمِسح .
The power and the generator are both out, so there's no elevator. Please take the stairs.	*-lkáhraba w -l[ᶠmoteur] tnaynētun maʔṭū3īn, fa-má fī [ᶠascenseur]. [please] ṭlá3i 3a-ddáraj.*	الكهْربا والموْتور تْنَيْناتُن مقْطوعين، فما في أسانْسور. پْليز طْلعي عالدّرج .
Do you have someone who can give you a ride to the next house [that you're cleaning]?	*3índik ħáda ywáṣṣlik 3a-lbēt ittēni?*	عِنْدِك حدا يْوَصِّلك عالبيْت التّاني؟

Do you charge by the hour, or by the visit? Do I get a discount if I make several bookings?	*btíʔbaḍi 3a-ssē3a aw 3a-zzyāra? btá3mli xáṣim íza bíɦjiz káza ɦájiz?*	بْتِقْبْضي عالسّاعة أَوْ عالزِّيارة؟ بْتعْمْلي خصِم إذا بِحْجز كذا حجِز؟
The bus will drop the kids off while you're here. Do you mind heading outside at 2:30 to greet them and bring them in, so that they're not alone?	*-lbāṣ raɦ yjīb liwlēd ínti w hōn. 3índik míškli trūɦi la-bárra -ssē3a tnēn w nuṣṣ tistaʔblíyun w tfawwtíyun, ta-má ykūnu wáɦdun?*	الباص رح يْجيب الوْلاد إنْتي وهوْن. عِنْدِك مِشْكْلِة تْروحي لبرّا السّاعة تْنيْن ونُصّ تِسْتقْبْلِيْنُ وتْفوّْتِيْنُ، تما يْكونوا وَحْدُن؟
Do you know how to cook Lebanese food?	*btá3rfi tíṭbxi ákil libnēni?*	بْتعْرْفي تِطْبْخي أكِل لِبْناني؟

Laundry and Tailoring بِالمصْبغة وعِنْد الخيّاط

For the average Lebanese, a مصْبغة *máṣbaɣa* **laundry shop/dry cleaner** is not a big part of everyday life, as pretty much all the washing, drying, and folding happens at home–if not by yourself, but your housekeeper. So, don't be surprised if you inquire after a laundry shop to someone in your neighborhood and they're not entirely sure where the closest one is. That does not mean that there isn't one nearby. It could very well mean that they simply have never had a use for one. For those who have the means, however, laundry shops are an essential part of their routine. You can take in your laundry and pick it up yourself or have it picked up and delivered back to your home. In small towns, it's typical for people to be loyal customers of the same laundry shop for decades and build a strong rapport.

GETTING CLOTHES IRONED

○ فيك پْليز تِكْويلي هَيْدا البَنْطلوْن؟
◇ أكيد بِأمْرك[1]. شو العِنْوان؟
○ البِنايِة اللي دِغْري بِوِجّك[2]. الطّابِق العاشِر. الشِّقّة رقِم تْنعْش.
◇ أوْكيْ، بِتْكون بِشِقّتك اللَّيْلِة، إذا الله راد.

○ Could you please iron this pair of pants?
◇ Of course. Your wishes are my command! What is the address?
○ The building right across [the street] from you, 10th floor, apartment number 12.
◇ Okay, it will be at your place this evening, God willing.

○ *fīk [please] tikwīli háyda -lbanṭalōn?*
◇ *akīd bi-ámrak[1]. šū -l3inwēn?*
○ *-lbinēyi -lli díɣri bi-wíjjak[2]. -ṭṭābiʔ il3āšir. -ššíʔʔa ráʔim tna3š.*
◇ *okē, bitkūn bi-šíʔʔtak illáyli, íza álla rād.*

[1] = تِكْرم عَيْنك *tíkram 3áynak*

[2] = مْقابيلك *mʔābīlak*

2

GETTING CLOTHES WASHED AND IRONED

○ مرْحبا، بسّ خوْد هَوْدي القُمْصان وقِلّو بدّي ياهُن قبْل الخميس.[1]

◇ تِكْرم عَيْنك ريِّس. بِترْيد شي تاني؟[2]

○ أيْه بسّ خلّيْن يْحُطّوْن عَ تعاليق. إذا طَوُوْن، بْيِتْطعْوَجوا.

◇ تحِت أمْرك[4] ريِّس.

○ Hi. Just take these shirts, and tell him I need them before Thursday.

◇ Of course, sir. Anything else?

○ Yes, please, bring them on hangers, not folded because the creases [from folding] would be visible.

◇ My pleasure!

○ *márɦaba, bass xōd háwdi -lʔumṣān w ʔíllu báddi yēhun ʔabl ilxamīs.*[1]

◇ *tíkram 3áynak ráyyis. bitrīd šī tēni?*[2]

○ *ē, bass xallíyun yɦuṭṭúwun 3a ta3ālīʔ. íza ṭawúwun, byitṭá3waju.*

◇ *táɦit ámrak*[4]*, ráyyis.*

[1] = وَدّيلو هوْل الِثّْياب وخبْرو إنّو مِسْتعْجِل عْلَيْهُن قبْل الخمِيس. *waddīlu hōl lityēb w xábbru ínnu mistá3gil 3láyhun ʔabl ilxamīs.*

[2] = بْتِؤْمُرْني بْشي تاني؟ *btiʔmúrni b-šī tēni?*

[4] = تِكْرم عَيْنك *tíkram 3áynak*

3

Having a suit cleaned

o هَيْدي البدْلِة يَلّي قصّرْتِلي ياها بدّا مصْبغة لإِنّو عِنْدي عِرِس بُكْرا.

◇ ما عِنّا مصْبغة بسّ فِيي غسِّلّك وإكْويلك ياها.

o أوْكي، بسّ عْموْل معْروف نْتبِه عْلَيا لإِنّو لازِم تِتْغسّل بمِيّ بارْدِة.[1]

◇ وَلا يْهِمّك رح إهْتمّ فِيا.

o I want to dry clean this suit that you took in, as I have a wedding [to attend] tomorrow.

◇ I don't have dry cleaning, but I'll clean and iron it for you.

o Okay, but please be careful with it as the material must be washed in cold water.

◇ Don't worry. I'll take care of it.

o *háydi -lbádli yálli ʔaṣṣartíli yēha bádda máṣbaɣa li-ánnu 3índi 3íris búkra.*

◇ *ma 3ínna máṣbaɣa bass fíyi ɣassíllak w ikwīlak yēha.*

o *okē, bass 3mōl ma3rūf ntíbih 3láya li-ánnu lēzim tityással bi-máyy bērdi.*[1]

◇ *wála yhímmak raḥ ihtámm fíya.*

[1] اه لأ ما رح يمْشي الحال. هَيْدي بدّا مصْبغة. *āh laʔ, ma raḥ yímši -lḥāl. háydi bádda máṣbaɣa.* **Oh, that's not going to work. This has to be dry-cleaned.**

[2] ما تِعْتل همّ. رح زبِّطْلك هِيّ. = *ma tí3tal hamm. raḥ ẓabbíṭlak* (here, هِيّ *híyyi* = ياها *yēha)*

4

GETTING A STAIN REMOVED

◇ هَيْدي البِقْعة صعْبِة تْروح.

o ليْه؟[1]

◇ لِأنّو كْلوْر، وديْجا أكل[2] اللّوْن.

o طيِّب، فينا نِصْبغا؟

◇ أيْه، بسّ بيكون اللّوْن أغْمق.

◇ This stain is difficult to get out.

o How come?

◇ Because it's chlorine, and it already ate away the original color.

o Well, can we dye it?

◇ Yes, but it will be a darker color.

◇ *háydi -lbíʔ3a ṣá3bi trūḥ.*

o *lē?*[1]

◇ *li-ánnu klōr, w [Fdéjà] ákal*[2] *illōn.*

o *ṭáyyib, fīna níṣbaɣa?*

◇ *ē, bass bikūn illōn áɣmaʔ.*

[1] = ليْش *lēš* (ليْه *lē* is more common in Beirut; ليْش *lēš* is more common in the north of Lebanon.)

[2] = سبق وأكل *sábaʔ w ákal*

5

Getting Clothing Altered (1)

o مرْحبا. بدّي قصِّر هَيْدا الفِسْطان عْمِلي معْروف.

◇ أوْكي. قدّيْ بِتْحِبّي تْقصّْريه؟

o علّمْتلِّك المطْرح بِدبابيس. بسّ بدّي إتْأكّد ما إضْطرّ غسّْلو بِسّ يِخْلص[1].

◇ وَلا يْهِمّك. مِنْغسِّل كمان. فبسّ خلِّص تقْصير، بْغسّْلو وبِكْويلِك ياه.

o مرْسي كْتير![2]

o Hello! I'd like to have this dress shortened, please.

◇ Okay, how much should I shorten it?

o I've marked the length with some pins, but I need to make sure I won't need to wash it afterward.

◇ Don't worry. We'll launder it, too. I'll just shorten it, then wash and iron it.

o Thanks a million!

o *márḫaba. báddi ʔáṣṣir háyda -lfisṭān 3míli ma3rūf.*

◇ *okē. ʔaddē bitḫíbbi tʔaṣṣrī?*

o *3allamtíllik ilmáṭraḫ bi-dbēbīs. bass báddi atʔákkad ma iḍṭárr ɣásslu bass yíxlaṣ*[1].

◇ *wála yhímmik. minɣássil kamēn. fa-báss xálliṣ taʔṣīr, byɣásslu w bikwīlik yēh.*

o *[Fmerci] ktīr!*[2]

[1] (lit. when it's finished); here, بسّ *bass* (+ imperfect verb) **as soon as**; more commonly, in other contexts, it can mean **but** or **just**. You can find examples of all three meanings in this dialogue.

[2] = يِسْلمو! *yíslamu!*

6

Getting clothing altered (2)

o بدّي ضيِّق هَيْدا القميص شْوَيّ.

◇ عِنْدِك واحد بِالقْياس اللي بدِّك ياه؟[1]

o أيْه، بِتْفضّْلي جيبنْ تْنَيْناتُنْ؟

◇ أيْه، أحْسن. وهيْك فِيي قِلِّك إذا بْيِتْضيّق أَوْ لأ.

o I want this blouse taken in a bit.

◇ Do you have another blouse in the size you want?

o Yes, should I bring them both?

◇ Yes, just bring both of them, and I'll let you know if it can be taken in or not.

o *báddi ḍáyyiʔ háyda -lʔamīṣ šwayy.*

◇ *3índik wāħad bi-liʔyēs -lli báddik yēh?*[1]

o *ē, bitfáḍḍli jību̱n tnaynētun?*

◇ *ē, áħsan. w hēk fíyi ʔíllik íza byitḍáyyaʔ aw laʔ.*

[1] عْطيني شي قميص مْنيح عْلَيْكي لضيِّق مِتْلو. *3ṭīni šī ʔamīṣ mnīħ 3láyki la-ḍáyyiʔ mítlu.* **Give me a shirt that fits you well so I can match it.**

○ بدّي صلّح كم شغْلِة إذا بتْريدي.

◇ أكيد دْموازيْل. تحت أمْرِك.[1]

○ فيكي ترْقّعي تْياب؟

◇ حسب الخِزِق أَوْ الفِخِت ونوْع القْماش.

○ أوْكيْ، فيكي تْشوفي هَيْدي الكنْزِة؟ عِلْقِت بمِسْمار ونْخزقِت.

◇ لأِنّو نايْلوْن، الطّريقة الوَحيدِة اللي فينا نْظبِّتا هِيِّ إنّو نْحُطّ رقْعة فوْق الخِزِق أَوْ نِطْرُز شي حَواليْه.

○ أوْكيْ، كيف بْتعْمْلي هيْك شي؟

◇ فِيي آخُد شقْفِة مْن الجيْبِة الجْوّانية، وأعْمِل جيْبِة برّانية هيْك شكِل تْغطّي الخِزِق.

○ أيْه فِكْرة كْتير مْنيحة. وبدّي كمان قصِّر هَيْدي التّنّورة وغيِّرْلا السّحّابِة.

◇ أوْكيْ، ما في مشْكل. شو كمان؟

○ آخِر شغْلِة، في هَيْدي الجاكيْتّ عْلَيا دِبِغ، ومِش عم بِقْدر قيمو.

◇ شو هَيْدا؟ زيْت أَوْ شو؟[2]

○ ما بعْرِف. بسّ جرّبِت كِلّ شي وما عم يِطْلع.[3]

◇ أوْكيْ، خلّيني جرِّب. بسّ في اِحْتِمال كْتير كْبير إنّو ما يِطْلع.

○ إذا صبغْناها، بْيِتْغطّى الدِّبِغ؟

◇ معْقول يْضلّ مْبينّ.

○ طيِّب، شوفي شو فيكي تعْمْلي وردِّي عْلَيي خبر.

◇ أوْكيْ، عْطيني رقِم تِلِفوْنك وبْقِلّك قبِل ما إصْبغ.

○ خِدي وَقْتِك فِيْن. الشّي الوَحيد اللي بدّي ياه عالسّريع هُوِّ هَيْدا الانْسامْبْل. بدّو مصْبغة[4] وكَوي.

◇ فينا نْسلْمِك ياه بعْد بُكْرا الصُّبِح، مْنيح هيْك؟

○ لأ، بُكْرا بِاللّيْل مكْسيموم وَلَوْ.[5]

◇ طيِّب، تِكْرم عَيْنِك.

○ I have a couple of things that need to be fixed.

◇ Certainly, miss. I'm at your service.

○ Do you do patches?

◇ It depends on the type of tear/hole and the fabric.

○ Okay, can you check this sweater? It got snagged on a pin and has this rip.

◇ Because it's nylon, the only way I can think of is sticking a patch on top of the rip, or we can sew a pattern or something around it.

○ All right, how would you go about it?

◇ I can take a part from the internal pocket and sew a little external pocket to hide this rip.

○ That's a good idea! All right. And I wanted to shorten this skirt and replace its zipper.

◇ Okay, no problem. What else?

○ One last thing: this jacket has this stain on it, and I have no idea how to get it out.

◇ Is it an oil stain or what?

○ I have no idea. I tried all sorts of things, and it won't come out.

◇ Let me try and see, but there's a good chance it might not come out.

○ If we dyed it, would it be concealed?

◇ It might be still visible.

○ Well, just see what you can do and let me know.

◇ Okay, give me your phone number, and I'll let you know before I dye it.

○ Take your time on these; they're not urgent. But more urgently, I need this outfit to be dry cleaned and ironed.

◇ Okay, if we deliver it the day after tomorrow in the morning, will that be okay?
○ No, tomorrow night at the latest, please.
◇ Okay, you got it.

○ *báddi ṣálliḥ kam šáɣli íza bitrīdi.*
◇ *akīd, [Fdemoiselle]. táḥit ámrik.*[1]
○ *fīki tráʔʔ3i tyēb?*
◇ *ḥásab ilxíziʔ aw ilfíxit w nō3 liʔmēš.*
○ *okē, fīki tšūfi háydi -lkánziʔ 3ílʔit bi-mismār w nxázaʔit.*
◇ *li-ánnu [nylon], iṭṭarīʔa ilwaḥīdi -lli fīna nzábbita híyyi ínnu nḥuṭṭ ráʔ3a fō' ilxíziʔ aw níṭruz šī ḥawalē.*
○ *okē, kīf btá3mli hēk šī?*
◇ *fíyi ēxud šáʔfi mn iljáybi -ljuwwēniyyi, w á3mil jáybi barrāníyyi hēk šákil tɣáṭṭi -lxíziʔ.*
○ *ē, fíkra ktīr mnīḥa. w báddi kamēn ʔáṣṣir háydi -ttannūra w ɣáyyirla -ssaḥḥābi.*
◇ *okē, ma fī máškal. šū kamēn?*
○ *ēxir šáɣli, fī háydi -l[Fjaquette] 3láya díbiɣ, w miš 3am bíʔdar ʔīmu.*[2]
◇ *šū háyda? zēt aw šū?*
○ *ma bá3rif. bass jarrábit kill šī w ma 3am yíṭla3.*[3]
◇ *okē, xallīni járrib. bass fī iḥtimēl ktīr kbīr ínnu ma yíṭla3.*
○ *íza ṣabaɣnēha, byitɣáṭṭa iddíbiɣ?*
◇ *maʔūl yḍall mbáyyin.*
○ *ṭáyyib, šūfi šū fīki tá3mli w ríddi 3láyi xábar.*
◇ *okē, 3ṭīni ráʔim [Ftéléphone]ik w bʔíllik ʔábil ma íṣbaɣ.*
○ *xídi wáʔtik fíyun. -ššī -lwaḥīd -lli báddi yēh 3a-ssarī3 húwwi háyda -lʔ[ensemble]. báddu máṣbaɣa*[4] *w káwi.*
◇ *fīna nsállmik yēh ba3d búkra -ṣṣúbuḥ, mnīḥ hēk?*
○ *laʔ, búkra bi-llēl [maximum] waláw.*[5]
◇ *ṭáyyib, tíkram 3áynik.*

[1] = تِكْرِم عَيْنِك، أُمْرِيني؟ *tíkram 3áynik, ʔmurīni?*

[2] مِش عم يْروح *miš 3am yrūḥ* **it's not going to come out**

[3] حاوَلِت بِكِلّ الطُّرْق. ما في أمل! *ḥāwálit bi-kill iṭṭúruʔ. ma fī ámal.* **I've tried every way. There's no hope.**

[4] Although مصْبغة *máṣbaɣa* shares a root with صبغ *ṣábaɣ* **to dye**, it means **laundry (shop)**, not just a place for dying fabric.

[5] وَلَوْ *waláw,* here, is used as an imploration (begging); it can also be used as a response to a 'thank-you.'

Vocabulary

dry cleaning	*[dry clean]*	دْراي كْلين
laundry shop	*máṣbaɣa*	مصْبغة
laundry	*ɣasīl*	غسيل
to wash	*ɣásal (yíɣsil)*	غسل (يِغْسِل)
spot, stain	*bíʔ3a*	بِقْعة
to dye	*ṣábaɣ (yíṣbaɣ)*	صبغ (يِصْبغ)
dye, dying	*ṣábɣa*	صبْغة
to iron	*káwa (yíkwi)*	كَوى (يِكْوي)
ironing	*káwi*	كَوي
to fold	*ṭáwa (yíṭwi)*	طَوى (يِطْوي)
coat hanger	*ta3līʔa*	تعْليقة
tailor's	*xiyyāṭ*	خيّاط
stitching, sewing	*xyāṭa*	خْياطة
tear, rip, cut	*xíziʔ*	خِزِق
to patch	*ráʔʔa3 (yráʔʔi3)*	رقّع (يرقِّع)
button	*zirr (zrār)*	زِرّ (زْرار)
buttonhole	*3írwi*	عِرْوَة

zipper	*saḫḫāb*	سحّاب
tape measure	*māzūra*	مازورة
to take in (make smaller)	*ḍáyya? (yḍáyyi?)* *záɣɣar (yzáɣɣir)*	ضيّق (يْضيِّق) زغّر (يْزغِّر)
to let out (make larger)	*wássa3 (ywássi3)*	وَسّع (يْوَسِّع)
to lengthen	*ṭáwwal (yṭáwwil)*	طوّل (يْطوِّل)
shorten	*?áṣṣar (y?áṣṣir)*	قصّر (يْقصِّر)
shortening	*ta?ṣīr*	تقْصير
skirt	*tannūra (tnanīr)*	تنّورة (تْنانير)
pants	*banṭalōn* *[Fpantalon]*	بنْطلوْن پنْطلوْن
shorts	*[short]*	شوْرْت
shirt	*?amīṣ (?umṣān)*	قميص (قُمْصان)
blouse	*blūzi*	بْلوزِة
dress	*fisṭān (fasāṭīn)*	فِسْطان (فساطين)
suit	*bádli*	بدْلِة
skirt suit	*[Ftailleur]*	تايور
suit jacket	*[Fjaquette] -lbádli*	جاكيْتّ البدْلِة
jeans	*[jeans]*	جينْز
linen	*kittēn*	كِتّان
chiffon	*šīfōn*	شيفوْن
satin	*sātēn*	ساتيْن

velvet	*ħarīr*	حرير
headscarf	*ħjēb*	حْجاب
t-shirt	*[t-shirt]*	تيشيرْت
sweatshirt	*[sweatshirt]*	سْويتْشيرْت
sweater	*kánzi*	كنْزِة
jacket	*[ᶠjaquette] (jwēkīt)*	جاكيْتّ (جْواكيت)
coat	*mōntō (mōntōyēt)*	مونْتوْ (مونْتوْيات)

Expressions

There's still extra fabric inside, so we have room to take it out a bit.	*fi ʔmēš min júwwa, yá3ni má3na majēl nţáwwlu šwayy.*	في قْماش مِن جُوّا، يَعْني معْنا مجال نْطوّلو شْوَيّ.
Please, iron this pair of pants without a crease.	*[please] kwī háyda -lbanţalōn bála ţá3ji.*	پْليز كْوي هَيْدا البنْطلوْن بلا طعْجِة.
Don't push too hard while ironing the [shirt's] cuffs because the buttons get loose or come off this way.	*ma tíkbis ktīr ínta w 3am tíkwi likmēm li-ánnu lizzrār btírtixi aw btínfakk.*	ما تِكْبِس كْتير إنْتَ وعم تِكْوي الِكْمام لِأنّو الزِّرار بْترِتْخي أَوْ بْتِنْفكّ.
I need to have this dress taken in.	*báddi ḑáyyiʔ háyda -lfisţān.*	بدّي ضيِّق هَيْدا الفِسْطان.

I want you to go over the stitching on this embroidered patch because it’s starting to fall off.	*báddi tírja3 túʔṭub ittaṭrīz li-ánnu bállašu yūʔa3u.*	بدّي تِرْجع تُقْطُب التّطْريز لأِنّو بلّشوا يوقعوا.
I need this tear to be mended.	*báddi háyda -lxízіʔ yitẓábbaṭ.*	بدّي هَيْدا الخُزِق يِتْظبّط.
I need these ironed right away as I’m going out in an hour.	*báddi tikwīli háwdi 3a-ssarī3, [please], li-ánni ḍāhra bá3d sē3a.*	بدّي تِكْويلي هَوْدي عالسّريع پْليز، لأِنّي ضاهْرة بعْد ساعة.
The shirt got burned while you were ironing it.	*háyda -lʔamīṣ ḫtáraʔ ínta w 3am tikwī.*	هَيْدا القميص احْترق إنْتَ وعم تِكْوِيا.

At the Post Office بِالبريد

البريد *-lbarīd* **the post office** in Lebanon, also known as LibanPost, has branches throughout the country, including at malls and the Beirut-Rafic Hariri International Airport. Business hours differ depending on the branch you're visiting, so it's always best to check their website (www.libanpost.com), which offers useful information about their services and is available in both English and Arabic, making it easy to locate the information that you need. As is the case at most post offices around the world, you can buy stamps, mail documents and letters, send packages, etc. Depending on the branch, LibanPost also often has a few agents, on-site, from money wiring services companies, such as Western Union. If you want more secure, certified methods of sending documents or items abroad, you're better off using a private company which has offices in major cities, such as DHL, FedEx, or UPS.

Sending a package

- ○ بدّي عذّبِك[1]، بدّي إبْعت هَيْدا الپاكاج عَ فْرنْسا. قدّيْ بدّو وَقِت تَيوصل؟
- ◇ شو هُوِّ عالمظْبوط؟[2] كم كيلو؟
- ○ هِنِّ كذا شغْلِة، بسّ كِلُّن عَ بعْضُن تْلاتِة كيلو.
- ◇ إذا مْنِبْعتو بريد عادي، بْيوصل خِلال عِشْرين يوْم وبيكلِّف خمْسين ألْف ليرة.

- ○ Excuse me, I would like to send a package to France. How long will it take?
- ◇ What is it exactly? How many kilos?
- ○ It's a couple of things actually, but, all together it's around 3 kilos.
- ◇ By standard shipment, it will arrive within 20 days and will cost 50,000 L.L.

- ○ *báddi 3ázzbik*[1]*, báddi íb3at háyda -l[package] 3a fránsa. ʔaddē báddu wáʔit ta-yūṣal?*
- ◇ *šū húwwi 3a-lmaẓbūṭ?*[2] *kam kīlu?*
- ○ *hínni káza šáɣli, bass kíllun 3a bá3ḍun tlēti kīlu.*
- ◇ *íza mnib3átu barīd 3ādi, byūṣal xilēl 3išrīn yōm w bikállif xamsīn alf līra.*

[1] (lit. I need to disturb you) is a common expression used to interrupt someone to ask for something and implies 'I know I'm being a bother, but…' or 'Sorry to bother you, but…'. عذّب *3ázzab* can mean **to torture** in some contexts, but it's not so dramatic here.

[2] = عِبارة عن شو بالتِّحْديد؟ *3ibāra 3an šū bi-ttaђdīd?*

2

SENDING MONEY

○ بدّي إبْعت مصاري[1] بويْسْترْن يونْيون عَ أبو ظبي پْليز.

◇ قدّيْ بدّك تِبْعت؟[2]

○ ألْف وميتيْن وخمْسين دوْلار.

◇ بدّك تِدْفع عشْرة دوْلار رْسومات، وفِيُن يِسْحبُوُن اليوْم إذا بدُّن.

○ أوْكي، كْتير مْنيح. شو بدِّك منّي؟[3]

◇ بدّي إسِم المِسْتِلِم، وقِلُّن إنّو لازِم يْفرْجوا هَوِيِّتُن بسّ يْروحوا يِسْتِلْموا المصاري، ولازِم يْكون الإسِم عالهَوِية مكْتوب بِذات الطّريقة مِتِل اللي إنْتَ بْتعْطيني ياه.[4] وبدّي الپاسْپوْر تبعك كمان.

○ I would like to send money via Western Union to Abu Dhabi, please.

◇ How much do you want to send?

○ $1,250.00

◇ You will pay $10 in fees, and they can withdraw it today if they wish.

○ Okay, great. What do you need from me?

◇ I need the recipient's name, and tell them that, when they go to receive the money, they will have to provide their I.D., with a name that matches the spelling you give me now. I also need your I.D. or passport.

○ *báddi íb3at maṣāri[1] bi-[Western Union] 3a ábu ḍābi, [please].*

◇ *ʔaddē báddak tíb3at?[2]*

○ *alf w mitēn w xamsīn dólar.*

◇ *báddak tídfa3 3ášra dólar rsūmēt, w fíyun yisḥábuwun ilyōm íza báddun.*

○ *okē, ktīr mnīḥ. šū báddik mínni?[3]*

◇ *báddi ísim ilmistílim, w ʔíllun ínnu lēzim yfárju hawiyyítun bass yrūḥu yistílmu -lmaṣāri, w lēzim ykūn ilʔísim 3a-lhawíyyi maktūb bi-zēt iţţarīʔa mítil -lli ínta bta3ţīni yēh.*[4] *w báddi -lpaspōr tába3ak kamēn.*

[1] = أعْمِل حْوالِة *á3mil ɧwēli*

[2] قدّيْ المبْلغ؟ *ʔaddē -lmáblaɣ?* **What's the amount?**

[3] شو المُسْتندات المطْلوبِة؟ *šū -lmustanadēt ilmaţūbi?* **What are the required documents?**

[4] = إسْمُن عالهوية لازِم يْكون مْطابِق لَيَلي رح تعْطيني هُوِّ. *ísmun 3a-lhawíyyi lēzim ykūn mţābiʔ la-yálli raɧ ta3ţīni húwwi.* (here, هُوِّ *húwwi* = ياه *yēh*)

3

RENTING A POST OFFICE BOX

○ عفواً، بدّي إسْتأْجِر صنْدوق بريد. شو المطْلوب منّي؟[1]

◇ مية وستّعْشر ألْف وخمْسْمية ليرة اِشْتراك سنَوي، صورة عن هَويْتِك أَوْ پاسْپوْرك، ووَرْقةْ بوْل[2].

○ وأيْ متى بيصير فيي إسْتعْملو[3]؟

◇ دِغْري. غيِّري عِنْوان بريدِك لعِنْوان صنْدوق البريد بسّ تعْطيه لحدا، وبيصير فيكي تِسْتِلْمي عْليْه.

○ Excuse me, I want to rent a P.O. box. What is required?

◇ A 116,500 L.L. annual fee, a photocopy of your I.D./passport, and a stamp.

○ When can I start using it?

◇ Right away. Just change your mailing address to the P.O. box and start giving it out, and then you can start receiving [mail] there.

○ *3áfwan, báddi istáʔjir ṣandūʔ barīd. šū -lmaṭlūb mínni?*[1]

◇ *míyyi w sittá3šar alf w xamsmīt līra ištirāk sánawi, ṣūra 3an hawíytik aw paspōrik, w wárʔit bōl*[2].

○ *w áymata biṣīr fíyi istá3mlu*[3]*?*

◇ *díɣri. ɣáyyri 3inwēn barīdik la-3inwēn ṣandūʔ ilbarīd bass ta3ṭī la-ḫáda, w biṣīr fīki tistílmi 3lē.*

[1] = بدّي إشْترِك بِعِنْوان بريد. شو الوْراق المطْلوبِة؟ *báddi ištrik bi-3inwēn barīd. šū liwrāʔ ilmaṭlūbi?*

[2] = طابِع *ṭābi3*

[3] = ساري المفْعول؟ *sēri -lmaf3ūl* **valid**

Sending important documents

○ بدّي إبْعت هَوْدي الوْراق بريد سريع[1] پْليز.

◇ شِبّاك رقِم حْدعْش، مع مدام سامْيَة.

(goes to window 11)

○ عفْواً، بدّي إبْعت هَوْدي الوْراق بريد سريع عَ لنْدن.

◇ عِنّا طريقْتينْ. إمّا مْنبْعتُن بُكْرا الصُّبح وبْيوصلوا بعْد خمْس تِيّام[2]، وبيكلّفوكي خمْسين ألْف. أَوْ مْنبْعتُن اللَّيْلة وبْيوصلوا بُكْرا بآخِر النّهار، وبيكلّفوكي خمْسة وسِتّين ألْف.

○ بِبْعتُن اللَّيْلِة پْليز. بدّي ياهُن يوصلوا بِأقْرب وَقِت مُمْكِن[3].

○ I would like to send these papers express, please.

◇ Window 11, with Mrs. Samia.

(goes to window 11)

○ Excuse me, I need to send this to London express.

◇ We have two options: We can either send it off tomorrow morning, and it will arrive within 5 business days and cost 50,000 L.L.; or we can overnight it, so it would get there by the end of the day tomorrow but would cost 65,000 L.L.

○ I'll overnight it, please. I need it to get there as soon as possible.

○ *báddi íb3at háwdi -liwrāʔ barīd sarī3[1], [please].*

◇ *šibbēk ráʔim ɦda3š, ma3 [Fmadame] sāmya.*

(goes to window 11)

○ *3áfwan, báddi íb3at háwdi -liwrāʔ barīd sarī3 3a [London].*

◇ *3ínna ṭarīʔtēn. ímma mnib3átun búkra -ṣṣúbuɦ w byūṣalu ba3d xams tiyyēm[2], w bikallfūki xamsīn alf. aw mnib3átun illáyli w byūṣalu búkra bi-ēxir innhār, w bikallfūki xámsa w sittīn alf.*

○ *bíb3atun illáyli, [please]. báddi yēhun yūṣalu bi-áʔrab wáʔit múmkin[3].*

[1] = بريد مِسْتعْجِل *barīd mistá3jil* / [2] إيّام *iyyēm* is pronounced تِيّام *tiyyēm* after a number. / [3] = بِأقْصى سِرْعة *bi-áʔṣa sír3a*

5

Picking up a package

o طيِّب، الوَصِل بيقلّي إنّو العِلْبِة وِصْلِت عَ مركز البريد هَيْدا.

◇ برْكي تْأخّرْتي تتِجي وردّوه عالمركْز الأساسي للبريد، تَيرْجْعوه ليَلّي بعتْلِك ياها.

o لأ، المفْروض إنّو وِصْلِت مْبارِح.

◇ أوْكيْ، عْطيني الوَصِل وإسْمِك تشوف شو فينا نعْمِل.

o Okay, the receipt I have tells me that the box has arrived at this post office.

◇ Maybe you came late, so it has already been sent back to the central post office, so it can be returned to the sender.

o No, it supposedly arrived yesterday.

◇ Okay, just give me the receipt and your name, and let's see what can be done.

o *ṭáyyib, -lwáṣil biʔílli ínnu -l3ílbi wíṣlit 3a márkaz ilbarīd háyda.*

◇ *bárki tʔaxxárti ta-tíji w raddū 3a-lmárkaz ilʔasēsi la-lbarīd, ta-yrajj3ū la-yálli ba3átlik yēha.*

o *laʔ, -lmafrūḍ ínnu wíṣlit mbēriḥ.*

◇ *okē, 3ṭīni -lwáṣil w ísmik tašūf šū fīna ná3mil.*

○ عفْواً، بدّي إتْلقّى[1] مصاري[2] بِويْسْتْرْن يونْيون مِن واشِنْطُن دي سي.

◇ شو إسْمِك؟

○ مارِيا روْبِرْتْسون.

◇ أوْكيْ، هَوِيْتِك لَوْ سمحْتي ورقِم الاِسْتِلام.

○ تْفضّلي پاسْپوْري وهَيْدا الرّقِم.

◇ أوْكيْ دُمْوازيْل، وِصْلوا. عْطيني ثَواني بسّ وبْجِبْلِك المصاري.

(The customer waits.)

◇ هَوْدي المصاري[3] دُمْوازيْل.

○ بسّ كان مفْروض يوصلّي ألْف دوْلار، هَوْدي أقلّ[4].

◇ اللي بعتْلِك المصاري الأرْجح حمّلّك إنْتي الرُّسومات تبع الخِدْمِة.

○ اه أوْكيْ طيِّب. وإذا بدّي إبْعت مصاري لحدا تاني، قدّيْ بدُّن وَقِت؟

◇ فِيْن يِسْتِلْمُوْن بِذات النّْهار دُمْوازيْل.

○ أوْكيْ، وبعْد سُؤال. في ملفّات بدّي إبْعتُن عَ فْلوْريدا عالسّريع. قدّيْ بدُّن وَقِت تَيوصلوا؟

◇ أحْسن تِسْألي[5] عَ شِبّاك رقِم واحد.

○ أوْكيْ مرْسي كْتير.

(goes to window 1)

○ عفْواً، بدّي إبْعت ملفّات عَ فْلوْريدا بِأميرْكا. قدّيْ بدُّن وَقِت تَيوصلوا؟

◇ بدُّن وَحْدِة وعِشْرين[6] يوْم إذا بريد عادي، تْلات تِيّام[7] إذا بريد سريع، ونْهار واحد بِبريد اليوْم التّاني.

○ قدّيْ بيكلّْفوا هَوْدي؟

◇ كم وَرْقة وشو قْياسُن؟

o بسّ في أرْبع وْراق، A4.[8]

◇ رح يْكلّفوكي تْلاتين ألْف للبريد العادي، أرْبْعين ألْف للبريد السّريع، وخمْسة وخمْسين ألْف لبريد اليوْم الواحد.

o بِهالحالةِ، بِبْعتُن بريد سريع پْليز.[9]

o Excuse me, I am receiving a money transfer via Western Union from Washington DC.

◇ What's your name?

o Maria Robertson.

◇ Okay, your I.D., please, and the number they gave you for picking up the money.

o Here are my passport and the number.

◇ Okay, miss. It has arrived. Give me a few moments, and I'll get the money for you.

(The customer waits.)

◇ Here's your money, miss.

o But I was supposed to receive $1,000. This is less.

◇ The sender must have deferred the fees to you.

o Hmm... I see, okay. What if I need to send some money to someone else? How long will it take?

◇ They can receive it on the same day, miss.

o Okay. And one more question, please. If I need to send some important documents to Florida in the U.S., how long will it take?

◇ You had better ask at window 1.

o All right. Thanks a lot.

(goes to window 1)

o Excuse me, I need to send some urgent documents to Florida, USA. How long will it take?

◇ It will take 21 days by standard delivery, three days for express, and one day for overnight shipping

o How much are those?

◇ How many sheets of paper and what size?

o There are just 4 papers, A4.

◇ It will cost you around 30,000 L.L. for standard delivery, 40,000 L.L. for express, and 55,000 L.L. for overnight shipping.
○ In that case, I'll send it express, please.

○ 3áfwan, báddi itláʔʔa¹ maṣāri² bi-[Western Union] min [Washington, D.C.].
◇ šū ísmik?
○ [Maria Robertson].
◇ okē, hawíytik law samáħti w ráʔim ilʔistilēm.
○ tfáḍḍali paspōri w háyda -rráʔim.
◇ okē, [ᶠdemoiselle], wíšlu. 3ṭīni sawēni bass w bjíblik ilmaṣāri.

(The customer waits.)

◇ háwdi -lmaṣāri³, [ᶠdemoiselle].
○ bass kēn mafrūḍ yūṣalli alf dólar, háwdi aʔáll⁴.
◇ illi ba3átlik ilmaṣāri -lʔárjaħ ħammállik ínti -rrusūmēt tába3 ilxídmi.
○ āh okē ṭáyyib. w íza báddi íb3at maṣāri la-ħáda tēni, ʔaddē báddun wáʔit?
◇ fíyun yistilmúwun bi-zēt innhār, [ᶠdemoiselle].
○ okē, w ba3d suʔāl. fī malaffēt báddi ib3átun 3a [Florida] 3a-ssarī3. ʔaddē báddun wáʔit ta-yūṣalu?
◇ áħsan tísʔali⁵ 3a šibbēk ráʔim wāħad.
○ okē [ᶠmerci] ktīr.

(goes to window 1)

○ 3áfwan, báddi íb3at malaffēt 3a [Florida] bi-amērka. ʔaddē báddun wáʔit ta-yūṣalu?
◇ báddun wáħda w 3išrīn⁶ yōm íza barīd 3ādi, tlēt tiyyēm⁷ íza barīd sarī3, w nhār wāħad bi-barīd ilyōm ittēni.
○ ʔaddē bikállfu háwdi?
◇ kam wárʔa w šū ʔyēsun?
○ bass fī árba3 wrāʔ, [A4]⁸.
◇ raħ ykallfūki tlētīn alf la-lbarīd il3ādi, arb3īn alf la-lbarīd issarī3, w xámsa w xamsīn alf la-barīd ilyōm ilwāħad.
○ bi-ha-lħāli, bib3átun barīd sarī3, [please]⁹.

¹ = إسْتِلِم istílim

² = حْوالة ħwēli

³ = تْفَضّلي مِصْرِيّاتِك tfáḍḍali miṣriyyētik

126 | At the Post Office

[4] كأنّو المبْلغ ناقِص؟ *ka-ánnu -lmáblaɣ nāʔiṣ?* **Isn't the amount insufficient [less than it should be]?**

[5] = تِسْتفِسْري *tístafisri*

[6] وِحْدِة *wíђdi* **one** becomes وَحْدة *w<u>á</u>ђd<u>a</u>* in compound numbers (21, 31, 41, etc.).

[7] إيّام *iyyēm* is pronounced تِيّام *tiyyēm* after a number.

[8] A4 is the international standard size for copy paper and measures 8.27 x 11.69 inches.

[9] = إذا بِترْيدي *íza bitrīdi*

Vocabulary

postal office	*máktab (makētib) barīd*	مكْتب (مكاتِب) بريد
mail carrier	*sē3i barīd*	ساعي بريد
mail	*barīd*	بريد
letter	*risēli (rasēyil)*	رِسالِة (رسايِل)
registered mail	*barīd msájjal*	بريد مْسجّل
address	*3inwēn (3anēwīn)*	عِنْوان (عناوين)
to send	*bá3at (yíb3at)*	بعت (يِبْعت)
sender	*mŭrsil, ba3it*	مٌرْسِل، باعِت
recipient, addressee	*místlim, bā3tīnlu*	مِسْتلِم، باعْتينْلو
post card	*[ᶠcarte]* *[card] (krūti)*	كارْت كارْد (كْروتِة)
window	*šibbēk (šbēbīk)*	شِبّاك (شْبابيك)
stamp	*ṭābi3 (ṭawābi3)*	طابِع (طَوابِع)

to stamp (with a postmark)	*xítim (yíxtum)*	خِتِم (يِخْتُم)
fiscal stamp (to show payment)	*dámɣa*	دمْغة
envelope	*ẓárif (ẓrūfi)*	ظرِف (ظْروفِة)
shipping	*šáɧin*	شحِن
shipment	*šíɧni*	شِحْنِة
urgent, express	*mistá3jil*	مِسْتعْجِل
parcel, package	*ţárd (ţrūd)*	طرْد (طْرود)
amount (of money)	*máblaɣ*	مبْلغ
fees	*rsūm*	رْسوم
receiving	*istilēm*	اِسْتِلام
ID card	*hawíyyi* *tázkara* *biţāʔa*	هَوية تذكرة بِطاقة
proof of identity	*isbāt hawíyyi*	إثْبات هَوية
passport	*paspōr*	پاسْپوْر

Expressions

○		
Customs shouldn't be applied to this.	*ma fī júmruk 3lē háyda.*	ما في جُمْرُك عْليْه هَيْدا.
I got this as a gift.	*háydi ijítni hdíyyi.*	هَيْدي إجِتْني هْدية.
◇		
You see, this shipment was sent back to the main office.	*háydi -ššíḫni ríj3it 3a maktábna -rraʔīsi.*	هَيْدي الشِّحْنة رِجْعِت عَ مكْتبْنا الرّئيسي.
The address is incorrect.	*háyda -l3inwēn miš maẓbūṭ.*	هَيْدا العِنْوان مِش مظْبوط.
Double-check the address.	*tʔákkad mn il3inwēn.* *šáyyik il3inwēn.*	تْأكّد مْن العِنْوان. شيِّك العِنْوان.
You can pick it up at window 5.	*fīk tistílmu min šibbēk ráʔim xámsi.*	فيك تِسْتِلْمو مِن شِبّاك رقِم خمْسِة.
We have to unwrap this package for us to be able to send it.	*lēzim tšīl ittaɣlīf 3an il[package] ta-fīna níb3atu.*	لازِم تْشيل التّغْليف عن الپاكاج تفينا نِبْعتو.

At the Bank بِالبنْك

Foreigners residing in Lebanon, whether in a professional capacity or otherwise, can open bank accounts at any major bank. The account can be either a savings or checking account, and the rules are the same: you need to have your passport and your tax ID number. Some banks will also ask for your permanent address back home. Most banks will have at least a couple employees who speak English, so you should be able to discuss your finances in English if you feel like you need it. But the dialogues in this chapter should help you feel confident in your daily banking needs in Levantine Arabic.

1

Opening a Checking Account

○ بدّي إفْتح حْساب پْليز عِنْدْكُن بِالبنْك.

◇ حْساب جاري أَوْ حْساب تَوْفير إسْتاذ؟

○ بْفضِّل حْساب جاري.

◇ بِتْحِبّ الِحْساب يْكون بِاللّيرة أَوْ بِالدّوْلار؟

o دوْلار پْليز. لأِنّو بْروح وبِجي كْتير عَ أميرْكا. شو الإجْرائات والملفّات[1] المطْلوبِة؟

◇ بدّي مِنّك پاسْپوْرك بِالأوّل و رقِم التّعْريف الضّريبي و عِنْوانك بِبلدك. وبدّك تعْمِل ديپوْسِت[2] عالقليلِة ميتيْن دوْلار. الحْساب ما في علْيْه رْسومات سنَوية وبْيِجي مع دبِت كارْد بِبلاش[3]. في رْسومات إذا بدّك تاخُد كْرديت كارْد.

o I'd like to open an account with your bank, please.
◇ Checking or savings, sir?
o I'd prefer checking.
◇ Would you like the account to be in L.L. or USD?
o USD, please, since I travel back and forth to the U.S. quite frequently. What is the process, and what documents do you require?
◇ I would need your passport first. I'll also need your tax I.D. number and your address back home. Then, you will make a [minimum] deposit of $200. No annual fees on the account, and it comes with a complimentary debit card. There will be a fee associated with a credit card if you want one.

o *báddi íftaḫ ḫsēb [please] 3índkun bi-lbánk.*
◇ *ḫsēb jēri aw ḫsēb táwfīr istēz?*
o *bfáḍḍil ḫsēb jēri.*
◇ *bitḫíbb liḫsēb ykūn bi-llīra aw bi-ddólar?*
o *dólar, [please]. li-ánnu brūḫ w bíji ktīr 3a amērka. šū -lʔijrāʔāt w ilmalaffēt[1] ilmaṭlūbi?*
◇ *báddi mínnak paspōrak bi-lʔáwwal w ráʔim itta3rīf iḍḍarībi w 3inwēnak bi-báladak. w báddak tá3mil [deposit][2] 3a-lʔalīli mītēn dólar. liḫsēb ma fī 3lē rusūmēt sanawíyyi w byíji ma3 [debit card] bi-balēš[3]. fī rusūmēt íza báddak tēxud [credit card].*

[1] = المُسْتندات *-lmustanadēt*

[2] = إيداع *īdē3*

[3] = مجّاني *majjēni*

2

Opening an account

o صباح الخيرْ، بدّي إفْتح حْساب بِالدّوْلار عِنْدْكُن بِالبنْك.

◇ فيكي تِفْتحي حْساب إذا بِتْحُطّي تْلات مية دوْلار دِيپوْسِت[1].

o بْيِطْلعْلي عْليْه فايْدِة؟

◇ بسّ حْسابات التّوْفير بْيِطْلعْلِك عْلَيا فايْدِة. هيْك كان بدِّك؟[2]

o Good morning, I'd like to open a dollar account at your bank.

◇ You can open an account with a minimum deposit of $300.

o Does it pay interest?

◇ Only savings accounts pay interest. Is that what you're looking for?

o *ṣabāḫ ilxēr, báddi íftaḫ ḫsēb bi-ddólar 3índkun bi-lbánk.*

◇ *fīki tíftaḫi ḫsēb íza bitḫúṭṭi tlēt mīt dólar [deposit][1].*

o *byiṭlá3li 3lē fēydi?*

◇ *bass ḫsēbēt ittawfīr byiṭlá3lik 3láya fēydi. hēk kēn báddik?*[2]

[1] = إيداع *īdē3*

[2] أيْه إذا قرّرتِ تِفْتح حْساب تَوْفير. الفايْدِة ساعِتا بِتْكون بينْ الواحد والواحد ونُصّ بِالمية، وبْتِنْدفع بِآخِر السِّنِة. **Yes, if you choose to make it a savings account. The interest would then range from 1 to 1.5 percent, which is paid out at the end of the year.**

3

Making a transfer

o عْمِلي معْروف، بدّي حوِّل هَيْدا المبْلغ مِن هَيْدا لِحْساب لهَيْدا لِحْساب.

◇ بدّا شي يَوْمين تتْبيِّن المصاري[1].

o ما في شي طريقة أسْرع؟[2]

◇ فينا نِسْحب المصاري مِن حْساب ونْحُطّن بِالحْساب التّاني، شرْط يْكونوا لِحْسابان بِذاتِ[3] البنْك.

o Excuse me, I'd like to transfer this amount to this bank account.

◇ It will take around two days to be reflected.

o Isn't there any other quicker way?

◇ We can withdraw the money from one account, and then deposit it in the other account, as long as they're both with the same bank.

o *3míli ma3rūf, báddi ḫáwwil háyda -lmáblaɣ min háyda liḫsēb la-háyda liḫsēb.*

◇ *bádda šī yawmēn ta-tbáyyin ilmaṣāri.*[1]

o *ma fī šī ṭarīʔa ásra3?*[2]

◇ *fīna nísḫab ilmaṣāri min ḫsēb w nḫúṭṭun bi-lḫsēb ittēni, šarṭ ykūnu -liḫsēbēn bi-zēt*[3] *ilbánk.*

[1] = عمليّة التّحْويل بْتاخِدْلا يوْمين. *3amalíyyit ittiḫwīl btexidla yawmēn.* **It takes two days for the transfer.**

[2] أيْه أوْكي ما بِيؤَثِّر. *ê okē, ma biʔássir.* **Yeah, okay. No problem** (lit. it doesn't affect [anything]).

[3] = بِنفْس *bi-náfs*

Reporting a faulty bank card

o سوْري، كارْتي منّو ماشي.[1]

◇ لحْظة إسْتاذ، خلّيني شيِّكْلك ياه.[2]

o جرّبْتو عَ أكْتر مِن أيْ تي إم، بسّ وَلا عم يِسْحب وَلا عم يَعْمِل شي.[3]

◇ مظْبوط، شكْلو منْزوع. فينا نُطْلُب واحد تاني. لازِم يِجْهز مِن هلّق لجِمِعْتينْ[4]، وفيك تِسْتِلْمو مِن هوْن.

o لازِم إدْفع شي عْليْه؟[5]

◇ لأ إسْتاذ، ما بْتِدْفع شي. هالمرّة عْليْنا.

- o Excuse me, my card is not working.
- ◇ One moment, sir. I'll test it for you.
- o I have already tried it in more than one ATM, but it still won't withdraw or do anything.
- ◇ True... It seems to have been damaged. We can request a new one be issued. It would take two weeks for it to be ready, and you can pick it up here.
- o Do I have to pay anything for that?
- ◇ No, sir, there are no additional fees. This one's on us.

- o *[sorry], kārti mánnu mēši.*[1]
- ◇ *láḫẓa istēz, xallīni šayyíklak yēh.*[2]
- o *jarrábtu 3a áktar min [AṭM] bass wála 3am yísḫab wála 3am yá3mil šī*[3].
- ◇ *mazbūṭ, šáklu manzū3. fīna núṭlub wāḫad tēni. lēzim yíjhaz min hálla? la-jimi3tēn*[4], *w fīk tistílmu min hōn.*
- o *lēzim ídfa3 šī 3lē?*[5]
- ◇ *la? istēz, ma btídfa3 šī. ha-lmárra 3láyna.*

[1] بِطاقْتي مِش شغّالِة. *biṭā?ti miš šaɣɣāli.*

[2] = ثَواني لإتْأكّد. *sawēni, la-it?ákkad.*

[3] ما في فايْدِة *ma fī fāydi* **it's no use**

[4] = معك حقّ. هَيْقِتو خرْبان. رح قدِّمْلك عَ واحد تاني. بْياخِدْلو شي أُسْبوعيْن. *má3ak ɧa??. hay?ítu xarbēn. raɧ ?addímlak 3a wāɧad tēni. byēxídlu šī usbū3ēn.* **You're right. It seems it's broken. I'm going to issue you another one. It'll take about two weeks.**

[5] عْليْه رُسوم؟ *3lē rusūm?* **Are there fees for that?**

5

Changing money

○ بدّي صرِّف يورو، پْليز.[1]

◇ قدّيْ بدِّك تْصرّْفي؟[2]

○ معي ميتينْ يورو. قدّيْ بْيِطْلعوا بِاللِّبْناني؟

◇ بْيِطْلعوا تْلات مية وأرْبْعين ألْف وخمْسْمية.

○ أوْكيْ تْفْضّلي.

○ I would like to exchange some euros, please.

◇ How much do you want to exchange?

○ I have 200 euros. How many Lebanese lira would that make?

◇ Around 340,500 L.L.

○ Okay, here you are.

○ *báddi ṣárrif [euro], [please].*[1]

◇ *ʔaddē báddik tṣárrfi?*[2]

○ *má3i mītēn [euro]. ʔaddē byíṭla3u bi-llibnēni?*

◇ *byíṭla3u tlēt míyyi w arb3īn alf w xamsmíyyi.*

○ *okē tfáḍḍali.*

[1] بدّي إشْترْي دوْلارات. *báddi íštri dolarāt.*

[2] قدّيْ المبْلغ؟ *ʔaddē -lmáblaɣ?*

Extended Dialogue

○ فتحِت حْساب هوْن بِالبنْك شهِر الماضي، بسّ كِلّما جرِّب إسْحب ما بْتِظْبط.

◇ فِيي شوف الپاسْپوْر تبعِك پْليز؟

○ تْفضّلي. وهَيْدا رقِم حْسابي.

◇ أيْه مدام، مظبْوط. تْجمّد حْسابِك مْوَقّت، تكِنْتي جِبْتيلْنا كِلّ وْراقِك[1].

○ ما فْهِمِت. أيّا وْراق ناقْصة؟ ديْجا جِبْتِلْكُن پاسْپوْري.

◇ بعْد بسّ بدّنا رقْم التّعْريف الضّريبي تبعِك. الظّاهِر إنّو ما عِنّا ياه بِملفِّك.

○ غريب. ليْه ما حدا طلبا مِنّي بِوَقْتا؟[2]

◇ مْنِعْتِذِر مِنِّك إنّو ما نْتبهْنا قبِل مدام.

○ طيِّب، إذا بْجِبْلك ياه، بعْد قدّيْ وَقِت تَيْبطِّل مْجمّد حْسابي؟

◇ تاني يوْم مكْسيموم، مدام.

○ أوْكيْ، إذا هيْك، بُكْرا بْجِبْلِك الرّقِم. بدّي كمان تْحضّريلي دفْتر شيْكات.

◇ وَلا يْهِمِّك مدام. بْحضِّرْلِك الطّلب مِن هلّق تكِنْتي رْجِعْتي بُكْرا.

○ وبعْد شغْلِة بسّ. يمْكِن يْكون عِنْدي سفْرة بعْد شهِر. فِيي إشْتْري دوْلارات مْن البنْك؟

◇ أيْه أكيد!

○ تمام. أوْكيْ فإذاً. بِرْجع بُكْرا، إذا الله راد، ومِنْخلِّص هالإشْيا.

◇ رح كون ناطِرْتِك[3] مدام.

○ I opened an account with your bank last month, but when I try to make a withdrawal, it won't work.

◇ May I have your passport, please?

○ Here you are. And here's the account number.

◇ Yes, ma'am, that is correct. A temporary freeze has been put on your account until you bring in all your documents.

○ I don't understand. What documents are missing? I have already given you my passport.

◇ It's just that we still need your Tax ID Number. It doesn't seem like we have one on file.

○ That's strange. Why didn't anyone ask me for this at that time?

◇ We apologize for the oversight, ma'am.

○ Okay, if I bring that, how long will it take for my account to be unfrozen?

◇ By the next day at most, ma'am.

○ Okay, in that case, I'll get you the number tomorrow, but I'd also like to have a checkbook issued.

◇ No problem, ma'am. I'll prepare the request for you by the time you come in tomorrow.

○ And just one more thing: I might be going on a trip in a month. Can I buy dollars from the bank?

◇ Yes, certainly.

○ Great. Okay then, I'll come back tomorrow, God willing, and we'll get these done.

◇ I'll be waiting for you, ma'am.

○ *fatáɦit ɦsēb hōn bi-lbánk šáhir ilmāɖi, bass kíllma járrib ísɦab ma btíʐbaʈ.*

◇ *fíyi šūf ilpaspōr tába3ik, [please]?*

○ *tfáɖɖali. w háyda ráʔim ɦsēbi.*

◇ *ē, [[F]madame], maʐbūʈ. tjámmad ɦsēbik mwáʔʔat, ta-kínti jibtīlna kill wrāʔik*[1].

○ *ma fhímit. áyya wrāʔ nāʔʂa? [[F]déjà] jibtílkun paspōri.*

◇ *ba3d bass báddna ráʔm itta3rīf iɖɖarībi tába3ik. -ʐʐāhir ínnu ma 3ínna yēh bi-maláffik.*

○ *ɣarīb. lē ma ɦáda ʈálaba mínni bi-wáʔta?*[2]

◇ *mni3tízir mínnik ínnu ma ntabáhna ʔábil, [[F]madame].*

- ○ *ţáyyib, íza bjíblik yēh, ba3d ʔaddē wáʔit ta-ybáţţil mjámmad ɧsēbi?*
- ◇ *tēni yōm [maximum], [Fmadame].*
- ○ *okē, íza hēk, búkra bjíblik irráʔim. báddi kamēn tɧaḑḑrīli dáftar šēkēt.*
- ◇ *wála yhímmik, [Fmadame]. bɧaḑḑírlik iţţálab min hállaʔ ta-kínti rjí3ti búkra.*
- ○ *w ba3d šáɣli bass. yímkin ykūn 3índi sáfra ba3d šáhir. fíyi íštri dólarāt mn ilbánk?*
- ◇ *ē, akīd!*
- ○ *tamēm. okē fa-ízan. bírja3 búkra, íza álla rād, w minxálliş ha-lʔíšya.*
- ◇ *raɧ kūn nāţírtik*[3]*, [Fmadame].*

[1] لازِم تْحدِّثي معْلوماتِك. *lēzim tɧáddsi ma3lūmētik.* **You need to update your information.**

[2] بسّ ما حدا خبّرْني. *bass ma ɧáda xabbárni.* **But nobody told me.**

[3] = بِإنْتِظارِك *bi-intiẓārik*

Vocabulary

bank	*bank (bnūk)*	بنْك (بْنوك)
the central bank	*-lbank ilmárkazi*	البنْك المرْكزي
account	*ɧsēb*	حْساب
checking account	*ɧsēb jēri*	حْساب جاري
savings account	*ɧsēb tiwfīr*	حْساب تِوْفير
interest	*fēydi (fawēyid)*	فايْدِة (فَوايِد)
earnings	*arbēɧ*	أرْباح
returns	*3awēyid*	عَوايِد
monthly	*šáhri*	شهْري
quarterly	*ríbi3 sánawi*	ربِع سنَوي
annually	*sánawi*	سنَوي
[bank] card	*[^{F}carte], [card]*	كارْت، كارد
debit card	*[debit] [card]/[^{F}carte]*	ديبِت كارْد/كارْت
ATM card	*[^{F}carte]/[card] il[AṭM]*	كارْت/كارْد الأيْ تي إم
to withdraw	*sáɧab (yísɧab)*	سحب (يِسْحب)
withdrawal	*sáɧib*	سحِب
to deposit	*wáda3 (yūdi3)*	وَدع (يودِع)
deposit	*īdē3* *[deposit]*	إيداع ديپوسِت
transfer	*taɧwīl*	تحْويل
bank teller	*mwáẓẓaf bank*	مْوَظّف بنْك

bank manager	*mudīr bank*	مُدير بنْك
ATM machine	*[AṭM]*	أيْ تي إم
ID (card)	*hawíyyi* *tázkara* *biṭāʔa*	هوية تذْكرة بِطاقة
passport	*paspōr*	باسْبوْر
credit card	*[credit card]*	كْريْدِت كارْد
Visa card	*[ᶠcarte] vīza* *vīza [card]*	كارْت ڤيزا ڤيزا كارْد
Mastercard	*[MasterCard]*	ماسْتر كارْد
lira	*līra (līrāt)*	ليرة (ليرات)
dollar	*dólar*	دوْلار
euro	*yūrō*	يوروْ
pound	*ráṭil*	رطِل
riyal	*ryāl*	رْيال
dinar	*dīnār*	دينار
loan	*qárḍ (qrūḍ)*	قرْض (قْروض)
debt	*dēn (dyūn)*	ديْن (دْيون)
funding	*tamwīl*	تمْويل
installments, payments	*taʔsīṭ*	تقْسيط
request	*ṭálab*	طلب
signature	*imḍāʔ*	إمْضاء

information	*bayēnēt*	بَيانات
information	*ma3lūmēt*	معْلومات
customer service	*xídmit il3úmala* *xídmit izzabēyin*	خِدْمِةْ العُملا خِدْمِةْ الزّبايِن
customer service	*[customer service]*	كسْتومر سرْفِيس
call center	*[call center]* *márkaz il?ittiṣāl*	كول سِنْترِ مرْكز الإِتِّصال
activation	*taf3īl*	تفْعيل
bank statement	*kašf ɧsēb*	كشْف حْساب
address	*3inwēn (3nēwīn)*	عِنْوان (عناوين)
phone number	*ra?m/númrit [ᶠtéléphone]*	رقْم/نمْرِةْ تِلِفوْن
to save up, put aside	*jámma3 (yjámmi3)*	جمّع (يْجمِّع)

Expressions

What are the bank's business hours?	*min áyya sē3a la-áyya sē3a byíftaɧ ilbánk?*	مِن أيّا ساعة لأيّا ساعة بْيِفْتح البنْك؟
What is the call center's phone number?	*?áddē rá?m il[call center]?*	قدّيْ رقِم الكال سنْترِ؟
How can I activate this card?	*kīf fíyi fá33il háyda -l[ᶠcarte]?* *kīf fíyi mášši háyda -l[card]?*	كيف فِيي فعِّل هَيْدا الكارْت؟ كيف فِيي مشّي هَيْدا الكارْد؟

I transferred this amount three days ago, but it hasn't been deducted yet from my account.	*ɦawwálit háyda -lmáblaɣ min tlēt tiyyēm, bass ba3d ma nsáɦab min ɦsēbi.*	حوّلِت هَيْدا المبْلغ مِن تْلات تِيّام، بسّ بعْد ما انْسحب مِن حْسابي.
I haven't received bank statements two months in a row.	*íli šahrēn miš wāṣílli kášf ɦsēb.*	إلي شهْريْن مِش واصِلّي كشْف حْساب.
Excuse me, I want to update my mailing address on the system.	*law samáɦit, báddi ɣáyyir 3inwēni 3a-l[system].*	لَوْ سمحِت، بدّي غيِّر عِنْواني عالسيسْتِم.
I want to clear out this account and close it.	*law samáɦit, báddi fáḍḍi liɦsēb w sákkru.*	لَوْ سمحِت، بدّي فضّي الحْساب وسكّرو.

◇

You can contact customer service, sir.	*fīk tittíṣil bi-l[customer service], istēz.*	فيك تِتّصِل بِالكسْتومر سرْڤيس، إسْتاذ.
You should make payments before the 5th of the month.	*lēzim tídfa3/tsáddid ʔábil xámsi -ššáhir.*	لازِم تِدْفع/تْسدِّد قبِل خمْسِة الشّهِر.

Visiting a Museum بِالمتْحف

Lebanon has been the center of many civilizations over the ages and is still home to 18 religious sects, all of which make it culturally and historically rich. And this is reflected in its museums. The biggest متْحف *máthaf* **museum** in Lebanon is متْحف بَيْروت الوَطني *máthaf báyrūt ilwáṭani* **the National Museum of Beirut**, which, in and of itself, is a historical site, having been founded in 1919 and built in 1930. Contemporary art lovers should pay the Sursock Museum a visit, and those who love science should not miss the MIM Mineral Museum housed at the University of Saint Joseph. While smaller museums in secluded villages are not always well-maintained, they're still worth a visit. Who knows? You might discover gems that you wouldn't want to miss! In other words, don't be discouraged by a museum's outer appearance.

Asking about hours of operation

○ لَوْ سمحِت، أيّا إيّام فاتح المتْحف؟[1]
◇ كِلّ يوْم إلّا الأحد.[2]
○ أوْكي، ومِن أيّا ساعة لأيّا ساعة؟[3]
◇ مْن التِّسْعة الصُّبْح للخمْسِة العصِر.
○ مرْسي كْتير.

○ Excuse me, on which days is the museum open?
◇ Every day except for Sunday.
○ All right, and what are the opening hours?
◇ From 9 a.m. until 5 p.m.
○ Thanks a lot.

○ *law samáɦit, áyya iyyēm fētiɦ ilmátɦaf?*[1]
◇ *kill yōm ílla -lʔáɦad.*[2]
○ *okē, w min áyya sē3a la-áyya sē3a?*[3]
◇ *mn ittís3a iṣṣúbuɦ la-lxámsi -l3áṣir.*
○ *[Fmerci] ktīr.*

[1] كيف أَوْقات المتْحف؟ *kīf awʔēt ilmátɦaf?* **What are the museum's hours?**

[2] = كِلّ إيّام الأُسْبوع ما عدا الأحد. *kill iyyēm ilʔusbū3 ma 3áda -lʔáɦad.*

[3] = و شو الدَّوام؟ *w šū -ddawēm?*

2

GOING THROUGH SECURITY

◇ پْليز حُطّ الشّنْطة عالمكنة، وحُطّ المفاتيح والسيْلوليرْ بِقلْب الشّنْطة.

o أوْكي ومِن ويْن فِيي جيب تيكِت لَوْ سمحْت؟[1]

◇ شِبّاك التّذاكر هونيك قبْل البوّابِة والأسْعار مكْتوبين فوْق الشِّبّاك.

◇ Please, put the bag in the [x-ray] machine, and put any keys or cellphone inside the bag.

o Okay. And where can I get tickets, please?

◇ The ticket window is over there before the gate, and the prices are written above the window.

◇ *[please] ɧuţţ iššánţa 3a-lmákana, w ɧuţţ ilmafatīɧ w il[F cellulaire] bi-ʔálb iššánţa.*

o *okē w min wēn fíyi jīb [ticket] law samáɧt?*[1]

◇ *šibbēk ittazēkar hunīk ʔábl ilbawwēbi w ilʔas3ār maktūbīn fōʔ iššibbēk.*

[1] لازِم إشْلح السّاعة و حُطّا عالمكنة كمان؟ *lēzim íšlaɧ issē3a w ɧúţţa 3a-lmákana kamēn?* **Should I remove my watch too and put it on the machine?**

3

Taking photos

◇ لَوْ سمحْت، التّصْوير مع فْلاش مِش مسْموح.

o بسّ شايِف غَيْري عم بيصوّروا عادي وما حدا عم بيقِلُّن شي.

◇ كانوا عم يِسْتعْمْلوا فْلاش قبِل وقِلْتِلُن ذات الشّي. عْمْوْل معْروف طِفّي[1] الفِلاش.

o طيِّب، أوْكي، رح إطْفيه[1].

◇ Excuse me, taking photos with flash is not allowed.

o But I can see others taking photos, and nobody has said anything to them.

◇ They were using flash earlier, and I told them the same thing. So, please turn your flash off.

o Okay, fine. I will.

◇ *law samáḫt, ittaşwīr ma3 [flash] miš masmūḫ.*

o *bass šēyif ɣáyri 3am bişáwwru 3ādi w ma ḫáda 3am biʔíllun šī.*

◇ *kēnu 3am yistá3mlu [flash] ʔábil w ʔiltílun zēt iššī. 3mōl ma3rūf, ţáffi[1] li[flash].*

o *ţáyyib, okē, raḫ íţfī[1].*

[1] طفّى (يْطفّي) *ţáffa (yţáffi)* and طفى (يِطْفي) *ţáfa (yíţfi)* are synonymous and both mean **to turn off** (a light, device); **to extinguish** (a fire, candle). The antonym of the first meaning is شغل (يِشْغِل) *šáɣal (yíšɣil)* **to turn on**.

Photography is allowed at museums, unless otherwise noted, but flash photography is normally not permitted. Tripods are generally not allowed, so it's better to check if you're bringing one along!

4

GETTING A TOUR GUIDE

○ عفْواً، في شي غَيْد يَعْمِلْنا تور للمتْحف؟

◇ في مْوَظّف فِي[1] يَعْمِلْكُن تور بعْد نُصّ ساعة.

○ أوْكيْ. رح تْكون بِالعربي؟ ولّا بْتِنْعمل كمان بِلُغات تانْيِة؟

◇ هِيِّ بسّ بِالعربي، بسّ في حدا يْترْجِمْلْكُن للإنْجْليزي.

○ أوْكيْ، بيكون كْتير مْنيح.

○ Excuse me, is there a tour guide that can give us a tour of the museum?

◇ There is an employee who can give you a tour in 30 minutes

○ All right. Will it be in Arabic, or is it available in other languages?

◇ Well, it's only done in Arabic, but someone else can translate it into English.

○ That would be great.

○ *3áfwan, fī šī [guide] yá3milna [tour] la-lmátђaf?*

◇ *fī mwáẓẓaf fị̄[1] yá3milkun [tour] ba3d nuṣṣ sē3a.*

○ *okē. raђ tkūn bi-l3árabi? wílla btin3ámal kamēn bi-luɣāt tēnyi?*

◇ *híyyi bass bi-l3árabi, bass fī ђáda ytarjímlkun la-lʔinglīzi.*

○ *okē, bikūn ktīr mnīђ.*

[1] في *fī* appears twice in this sentence. The first is the more common **there is/are**, while the second is a variant form of فِيو *fíyu* **he can**.

5

Asking where an exhibit is located

○ عفْواً، ويْن غْراض جِبْران خليل جِبْران؟

◇ محْطوطين بِآخِر طابِق مع تابوتو.

○ اه أوْكي، وكيف فِي أوصل عْلينّ. ويْن الدّرج؟ بدّي تيكِت تاني؟[1]

◇ الدّرج مِن هوْن.[2] فيكي تِسْتعْمْلي ذات التّذْكره اللي معِك.

- ○ Excuse me, where are the belongings of Gibran Khalil Gibran?
- ◇ Those are on the top floor of the museum, along with his casket.
- ○ Oh okay. How do I get there? Where are the stairs? And do I need a different ticket?
- ◇ The stairs are right this way, and you can use the same ticket you already bought.

- ○ *3áfwan, wēn ɣrāḏ jibrān xalīl jibrān?*
- ◇ *maɦṭūṭīn bi-ēxir ṭābiʔ ma3 tēbūtu.*
- ○ *āh okē, w kīf fíyi ūṣal 3láyyun. wēn iddáraj? báddi [ticket] tēni?*[1]
- ◇ *-ddáraj min hōn.*[2] *fīki tistá3mli zēt ittázkara -lli má3ik.*

[1] وِيْن المدْخل؟ فِي فوت بِذات التّذْكرة؟ *wēn ilmádxal? fíyi fūt bi-zēt ittázkara?* **Where is the entrance? Can I go in without a [special] ticket?**

[2] الدّخْلِة مِن هَيْدي الميْلِة. *-ddáxli min háydi -lmáyli.* **The entrance is on this side.**

6

ASKING SOMEONE TO TAKE YOUR PICTURE

○ فيك تْصوِّرْنا صورة پْليز؟[1]

◇ أكيد! بِتْحِبّي صوِّرا بِالطّول أَوْ بِالعرِض؟

○ بِالطّول پْليز أحْسن. وپْليز تْكون الِكْنيسِة اللي وَرانا مْبيِّنة.[2]

◇ تِكْرم عَيْنِك. صوَّرِت كم صورة هيْك. فيكي تْنقّي اللي بْتِعْجْبِك.

○ مرْسي كْتير!

○ Can you take a photo for us, please?

◇ Sure! Do you want it portrait or landscape?

○ Portrait would be better. And please make sure that chapel is included.

◇ My pleasure... I took a couple of photos so you can choose.

○ Thank you very much.

○ *fīk tṣawwírna ṣūra, [please]?*[1]

◇ *akīd! bitḫíbbi ṣáwwira bi-ṭṭūl aw bi-l3áriḍ?*

○ *bi-ṭṭūl [please] áḫsan. w [please], tkūn liknīsi -lli warāna mbáyyni.*[2]

◇ *tíkram 3áynik. ṣawwárit kam ṣūra hēk. fīki tnáʔʔi -lli btí3jbik.*

○ *[ᶠmerci] ktīr!*

[1] = فيك تاخِدِلّنا صورة؟ *fīk tēxidíllna ṣūra?*

[2] = طلِّع الِكْنيسِة بِالصّورة پْليز. *ṭálli3 liknīsi bi-ṣṣūra, [please].* **Get the church in the picture, please.**

○ لَوْ سمحْتي، البِطاقات تبع الوِلاد ذات الشّي مِتِل تبع الكِبار؟[1]

◇ للتّلاميذ اللِّبْنانية خمْسْتلاف، التّلاميذ الأجانِب عشِرْتلاف. للبْنانية الكِبار تمْانْتلاف، والأجانِب الكِبار تْنعْشر ألْف. الوِلاد اللي أزْغر مِن أرْبع سْنين بيفوتوا بِبلاش.

○ أوْكيْ، بدْنا نِشْتري تذْكرْتيْن للأجانِب، ومعْنا كمان زلمِة لِبْناني مع إبْنو عُمْرو تْلات سْنين.

◇ أوْكيْ، المجْموع تْنيْن وتْلاتين ألْف.

○ أوْكي تْفضّلي.

◇ أوْكيْ، پْليز نْطْري هوْن تجبْلِك فْراطة ردِّلِك.

○ المتْحف بْيِفْتح كِلّ يوْم؟[2]

◇ أيْه بْيِفْتح كِلّ يوْم.

○ يَعْني إذا جينا نْهار سبِت بيكون فاتح عادي؟[3]

◇ أيْه فاتح السّبِت، بسّ أحْسن إذا بْتِجي العصِر، بِتْكون خفِّةْ العجْقة.

○ فينا نْصوِّر جُوّا وِلّا ممْنوع؟

◇ لأ التّصْوير جُوّا مِش مسْموح لِأنّو الفْلاش بيأثِّر عالتّحف.

○ أوْكيْ، بدّي أعْرِف كمان إذا في حدا يَعْمِلْنا تور[4].

◇ كِلّ تِحْفِة فِيا معْلومات تحْتا بِالعربي وبِالإنْجْليزي.

○ وشو هَيْدا التِّمْثال اللي برّا؟ هَيْدا مْن الآثارات وِلّا بِنْيوه بْهالقُرْب تَيْكرْموا شخْصية تاريخية.

◇ هَيْدا تمِْثال بْشارة الخوري. بِنْيوه بِالتِّسْعينات مِن بعْد ما مات بِكْتير.

○ مين بْشارة الخوري؟

◇ كان أوّل رئيس جُمْهورية مِن بعْد اِسْتِقْلال لِبْنان. لِعِب دوْر كْبير بِالاِسْتِقْلال.

- o Excuse me, are the tickets for children the same as for adults?
- ◇ For Lebanese students 5,000 L.L., foreign students 10,000 L.L. For Lebanese adults, 8,000 L.L., and foreigners 12,000 L.L. Kids under four years old enter for free.
- o Okay, we would like to buy two adult tickets for foreigners, and we also have a Lebanese man with his child, who is three years old.
- ◇ Then the total will be 32,000 L.L.
- o Okay, here you are.
- ◇ Okay, please wait here until I find you some change.
- o Is the museum open every day?
- ◇ Yes, it is open every day.
- o So, if we came on a Saturday, would it be open as usual?
- ◇ Yes, it's open on Saturdays, but it's best if you come late afternoon; it's less crowded.
- o Can we take photos inside, or is it not allowed?
- ◇ No, it's not allowed because the flash affects the antiquities.
- o All right. I'd also like to know if there's someone who can give us a tour.
- ◇ Well, every relic has its information written underneath it in Arabic and English.
- o What about this statue outside? Is it a monument [authentic] or was it built recently to honor a historical figure?
- ◇ It's the statue of Bechara EL-Khoury! It was built in the 90s, long after his death.
- o Who's Bechara El-Khoury?
- ◇ He was the first Lebanese president post-independence, in which he played a key role.

- o *law samáħti, -lbiṭāʔāt tába3 liwlēd zēt iššī mítil tába3 likbār?*[1]

◇ *la-ttalēmīz illibnēníyyi xamstalēf, -ttalēmīz ilʔajēnib 3aširtalēf. la-libnēníyyi likbār tmēntalēf, w ilʔajēnib likbār tná3šar alf. liwlēd -lli ázɣar min árba3 snīn bifūtu bi-balēš.*

○ *okē, báddna níštri tazkartēn la-lʔajēnib, w má3na kamēn zálami libnēni ma3 íbnu 3úmru tlēt snīn.*

◇ *okē, -lmajmū3 tnēn w tlētīn alf.*

○ *okē tfáḍḍali.*

◇ *okē, [please] nṭúri hōn ta-jíblik frāṭa riddílik.*

○ *-lmátħaf byíftaħ kill yōm?*[2]

◇ *ē, byíftaħ kill yōm.*

○ *yá3ni íza jīna nhār sábit bikūn fētiħ 3ādi?*[3]

◇ *ē, fētiħ issábit, bass áħsan íza btíji -l3áṣir, bitkūn xáffit il3ájʔa.*

○ *fīna nṣáwwir júwwa wílla mamnū3?*

◇ *laʔ -ttaṣwīr júwwa miš masmūħ li-ánnu li[flash] biʔássir 3a-ttíħaf.*

○ *okē, báddi á3rif kamēn íza fī ħáda ya3mílna [tour]*[4]*.*

◇ *kill tíħfi fíya ma3lūmēt táħta bi-l3árabi w bi-lʔinglīzi.*

○ *w šū háyda -ttimsēl -lli bárra? háyda min ilʔasārāt wílla binyū bi-ha-lʔúrub ta-ykárrmu šaxṣíyyi tērīxíyyi.*

◇ *háyda timsēl bšāra -lxūri. binyū bi-ttis3īnēt min ba3d ma mēt bi-ktīr.*

○ *mīn bšāra -lxūri?*

◇ *kēn áwwal raʔīs jumhūríyyi min ba3d istiʔlēl libnēn. lí3ib dōr kbīr bi-lʔistiʔlēl.*

[1] = الوِلاد و الكِبار نفْس الأسْعار؟ *liwlēd w likbār nafs ilʔas3ār?*

[2] كيف دَوام المتْحف؟ *kīf dawēm ilmátħaf?* **What are the museum's hours?**

[3] بْيِفْتح برّات الأُسْبوع؟ *byíftaħ barrāt ilʔusbū3?* **Is it open on weekends** (lit. outside the week)**?**

[4] = في عِنْكُن حدا يَعْمِلْنا بَرْمِة؟ *fī 3índkun ħáda ya3mílna bármi?*

Vocabulary

museum	*mátђaf (matēђif)*	متْحف (متاحِف)
gate	*buwwēbi*	بُوّابِة
entrance	*mádxal*	مدْخل
exit	*máxraj*	مخْرج
inspection	*tiftīš*	تِفْتيش
guard	*ђāris (ђirrās)*	حارِس (حِرّاس)
security	*[security]* *ámin*	سيْكوريتيْه أمِن
(food) containers	*[Tupperware]*	تاپيرْويْر
cellphone	*[Fcellulaire]*	سيْلوليرْ
window	*šibbēk (šbēbīk)*	شِبّاك (شْبابيك)
ticket	*tázkara (tazēkir)*	تذْكرة (تذاكِر)
guide	*[guide], muršid*	غيْد، مُرْشِد
tour	*[tour]* *jáwli* *bármi*	تور جَوْلِة برْمِة
photography	*taşwīr*	تصْوير
camera	*[camera]*	كاميرا
monument, relic, antiquity	*ásar (āsār)*	أثر (آثار)
historical	*ásari* *tērīxi*	أثري تاريخي

civilization, culture	*ḫaḍāra*	حضارة
period, era, age	*3áşir (3uşūr)*	عصِر (عُصور)
Roman	*rūmāni*	روماني
Islamic	*islēmi*	إسْلامي
Greek	*yūnēni*	يوناني
B.C.	*ʔabl ilmīlēd*	قبْل الميلاد
A.D.	*ba3d ilmīlēd*	بعْد الميلاد
statue	*timsēl (tamāsīl)*	تمِثْال (تماثيل)
column	*3amūd (3wēmīd)*	عمود (عْواميد)
weapons	*áslïḫa*	أسْلِحة
currency	*3ímli*	عِمْلِة
tools	*adawēt*	أدَوات
wooden	*xášab*	خشب
mask	*[mask]*	ماسْك
mausoleum, large tomb	*ḍarīḫ*	ضريح
tomb	*ʔábir (ʔbūr)*	قبِر (قْبور)
coffin	*tēbūt (twēbīt)*	تابوت (تْوابيت)
crown	*tēj*	تاج

Expressions

How long has this museum been open [to the public]?	*ʔaddē ílu -lmátḫaf fētiḫ?*	قدّيْ إلو المتْحف فاتح؟
Is there somewhere I can leave my belongings?	*fī šī máṭraḫ fíyi ítruk ɣrāḍi?*	في شي مطْرح فِيي إتْرُك غْراضي؟
I want two tickets for foreigners.	*báddi tazkartēn la-lʔajēnib.*	بدّي تذْكرْتيْن للأجانِب.
I want to buy an adult ticket.	*báddi íštri tázkara la-likbār.*	بدّي إشْتْري تذْكرة للِكْبار.
Can I wait for the next tour?	*fíyi intíẓir it[tour] ittēni?*	فِيي إنْتِظِر التّور التّاني؟

◇

No leaning on the glass.	*mamnū3 tílʔi 3a-liʔzēz.*	ممْنوع تِلْقي عالِقْزاز.
Photography without flash only.	*ittaṣwīr bála [flash].*	التّصْوير بلا فْلاش.
This museum is divided into three floors.	*háyda -lmátḫaf mʔássam 3a tlēt ṭawābiʔ.*	هَيْدا المتْحف مْقسّم عَ تْلات طَوابِق.
It's a historical palace that the state has turned into a museum.	*húwwi ʔáṣir ásari ḫawwalitū iddáwli la-mátḫaf.*	هُوِّ قصِر أثري حوّلِتوه الدَّوْلِة لمتْحف.

At a Mosque بِالجامع

Lebanon is home to 18 طايْفِة *ţāyfi* (طَوايف *ţawāyif)* **religious sects** that contribute to its cultural richness. This diversity means that you can find mosques and churches in abundance, and can even find Jewish temples (though rarer), in some areas. The most well-known mosques جَوامع *jawēmi3* (or مساجِد *masējid*) include Mohammad Al-Amin Mosque, Al Mansouri Mosque, and Al-Omari Grand Mosque. Non-Muslims can visit mosques as long as they respect the rules and etiquette, which are comparable to those of mosques elsewhere. It's best to visit outside of prayer times (although some mosques do allow visitors even during prayer time). Both men and women should be dressed modestly, or they will require that you wear a عبايِة *3abēyi* that they provide. Women should also cover their hair with a scarf, so you should either bring one with you or use one they provide you with. Photography is allowed inside most mosques outside of prayer times, but it is always better to ask and be on the safe side.

Looking for a Mosque

○ لَوْ سمحْتي، ويْن جامِع[1] السُّلْطان عبْدالمجيد؟

◇ بِتْضلِّك رايْحة دِغْري[2]، وبِتْلاقي بِآخِر الشّارِع. ما بِتْضيِّعيه، دِغْري حدّ[3] الِكْنيسِة. مِش منْظر بِتْشوفي كِلّ يوْم![4] هَيْدي شغْلِة مْن الإِشْيا اللي بْتعْمِل هالمدينِة فريدِة مِن نَوْعا.

○ واوْ حِلو كْتير! مرْسي كْتير!

◇ بسّ انْتِبْهي لازِم تْفوتي لابْسِة حْجاب.[5]

○ أيْه معي شال.

○ Excuse me, where is the Sultan Abdel Majid Mosque?

◇ Keep walking straight, and you'll find it at the end of the street. You can't miss it; it's right next to the church. It's not a common sight! One of the things that make this city so unique.

○ Wow - that's amazing. Thanks a lot!

◇ But keep in mind that you have to enter wearing hijab.

○ Yes, I have a scarf.

○ *law samáɦti, wēn jēmi3*[1] *issulţān 3abd ilmajīd?*

◇ *bitđállik rāyɦa díɣri*[2]*, w bitlēʔi bi-ēxir iššēri3. ma bitđayy3ī, díɣri ɦadd*[3] *liknīsi. miš mánẓar bitšūfi kill yōm!*[4] *háydi šáɣli mn ilʔíšya -lli btá3mil ha-lmadīni farīdi min náw3a.*

○ *wāw ɦilu ktīr! [Fmerci] ktīr!*

◇ *bass ntíbhi lēzim tfūti lēbsi ɦjēb.*[5]

○ *ē, má3i šēl.*

[1] = وِيْن صار جامع *wēn şār jēmi3*

[2] = عَ طول *3a ţūl*

[3] = جنْب *jamb*

4 = منْظر كْتير نادِر! *mánẓar ktīr nēdir!* **A rare sight!**

5 لازِم تْغطّي شعْرِك. *lēzim tɣáṭṭi šá3rik.* **You have to cover your hair.**

6 وِيْن فِيي إشْتْري طرْحة؟ *wēn fíyi íštri ṭárħa?* **Where can I buy a headscarf?**

This dialogue takes place in Byblos, where Sultan Abdel Majid Mosque is located. Another example of a church right next to a mosque St. George Maronite church and Mohammad Alamin Mosque in Beirut, which appear on the cover of this book.

The Mohammad Al-Amin Mosque is especially beautiful, and its architecture is often lauded. It has been supported generously by the Hariri family (which is the Prime Minister's family and a very prominent Sunni family with strong ties to Saudi Arabia), as Rafic El-Hariri (the former Lebanese Prime Minister, who was assassinated in 2005 and is the father of the current Prime Minister, Saad El-Hariri) is buried near the mosque.

2

DRESSING APPROPRIATELY FOR MEN

◇ ما فيك تْفوت بِالشّوْرْت إسْتاذ.

○ طب شو بدّي[1] أعْمِل؟ كيف فِيي غطّي؟

◇ فوت عَ إيدك اليَمين، تْروك بوْطك مع الزّلمي اللي هونيك، وبِتْلاقي كمان معو شي تْغطّي حالك فيه.

○ أوْكيْ، يِسْلمو.

◇ You can't enter with shorts, sir.

○ Well, what am I supposed to do? How can I cover up?

◇ Enter on the right, leave your shoes with that man over there, and you will find he has something you can use to cover yourself with.

○ Okay, thanks a lot.

◇ *ma fīk tfūt bi-š[short], istēz.*

○ *ṭab, šū báddi[1] á3mil? kīf fíyi ɣáṭṭi?*

◇ *fūt 3a īdak ilyamīn, trūk bōṭak ma3 izzálami -lli hunīk, w bitlēʔi kamēn má3u šī tɣáṭṭi ḥālak fī.*

○ *okē, yíslamu.*

[1] بدّو *báddu* normally translates as **want**, but here it implies a requirement/need and can translate **should**, **is supposed to**, **need to**.

3

DRESSING APPROPRIATELY FOR WOMEN

◇ ما فيكي تْفوتي هيْك يا سِتّ.[1]

o بسّ لابْسِة حْجاب!

◇ أيْه بسّ لابْسِة بنْطلوْن قدّ الجِسِم[2] كمان.

o طيِّب شو بدّي أعْمِل؟[3]

◇ فيكي تِسْتْعيري تنّورة طَويلِة أَوْ شادوْر مِن هونيك.

◇ You cannot enter like this, ma'am.
o But I'm wearing hijab!
◇ Yes, but you're wearing form-fitting pants.
o Well, what to do now?
◇ You can borrow a skirt or chador from over there.

◇ *ma fīki tfūti hēk ya sitt.*[1]
o *bass lēbsi ħjēb!*
◇ *ē, bass lēbsi banṭalōn ʔadd iljísim*[2] *kamēn.*
o *ṭáyyib šū báddi á3mil?*[3]
◇ *fīki tist3īri tannūra ṭawīli aw šādōr min hunīk.*

[1] لِبْسِك مِش مْطابِق للشُّروط مدام. *líbsik miš mṭābiʔ la-ššrūṭ [Fmadame].* **Your attire does not adhere to the regulations, ma'am.**

[2] ضيِّق *ḍáyyiʔ* **tight**

[3] – شو العمل؟ *šū -lʕamal?* = شو المطْلوب؟ *šū -lmaṭlūb?* (lit. What's required?)

Timing your visit

◇ سوْري ما فيك تْفوت هلّق. رْجعوا بعْد نُصّ ساعة، بسّ تِخْلص الصّلا.

○ ما فينا بسّ نْفوت عالسّاحة؟ ما مِنْفوت عَ قلْب الجامِع.

◇ لأ إسْتاذ. السُّوّاح يَلّي جايين يِتْفرّجوا ممْنوع يْفوتوا لِبعْد[1] الصّلا.

○ طيِّب، مْنرِجْع بعْد نُصّ ساعة.[2]

◇ Sorry, you can't go in now. Come back in 30 minutes when the prayers are over.

○ Can we just enter the courtyard area? We won't go inside the mosque.

◇ No, sir. Tourists who are here for sightseeing are not allowed in until after the prayers.

○ Okay, we'll come back in half an hour.

◇ *[sorry] ma fīk tfūt hálla?. rjá3u ba3d nuşş sē3a, bass tíxlaş işşála.*

○ *ma fīna bass nfūt 3a-ssēħa? ma minfūt 3a ʔálb iljēmi3.*

◇ *la?, istēz. -ssuwwēħ yálli jēyīn yitfarráju mamnū3 yfūtu la-bá3d[1] işşála.*

○ *ţáyyib, mnírja3 ba3d nuşş sē3a.[2]*

[1] لتِخْلص *la-tíxlaş* **until... finishes**

[2] رح ناخُد لكان لفّة حَوْل الجامع عَ بال ما تِخْلص الصّلا. *raħ nēxud lakēn láffi ħawl iljēmi3 3a bēl ma tíxlaş işşála.* **Then, we'll walk around [the outside of] the mosque until the prayer is over.**

5

Performing ablution

○ عفواً، ويْن فِيي إتْوَضّى؟[1]

◇ برّا، إذا بْتاخْدي يمين، بِتْلاقي محلّ الوُضوء.

○ أوْكي، يِسْلمو[2]!

◇ تِكْرمي. الله يِسْتقْبِل مِنِّك. وجِمْعة مْبارْكِة انْشالله.

○ Excuse me, where can I perform ablution?

◇ Outside. You will take a right, and you'll find the ablution area right there.

○ Okay, thanks a lot.

◇ You're welcome. May God accept your prayers, and have a blessed Friday, God willing.

○ *3áfwan, wēn fíyi itwáḍḍa?*[1]

◇ *bárra, íza btēxdi yamīn, bitlēʔi maɦáll ilwuḍūʔ.*

○ *okē, yíslamu*[2]*!*

◇ *tíkrami. álla yistáʔbil mínnik. w jím3a mbārki, nšálla.*

[1] وِيْن الحمّام إذا بِتْرِيد؟ *wēn ilɦammēm, iza bitrīd?* **Where's the washroom, please?**

[2] = شُكْراً *šúkran*

6

PRAYER SECTION FOR LADIES

○ لَوْ سمحِت، وِيْن مُصلّى السِّتّات.
◇ تاني باب عالشْمال. ثَواني وبِبْعت حدا يِفْتحْلِك الباب.
○ أوْكيْ، مرْسي. وفِيي شوف[1] الشّيْخ؟
◇ في شي مِشْكْلِة؟[2]
○ لأ بسّ بدّي إسْألو عن فتْوى.
◇ أوْكيْ لْحقيني وبْدِلّك عَ مكْتبو.

○ Excuse me, where is the prayer section for ladies?
◇ Through the next door on the left. Just a moment and I'll send someone to open the door for you.
○ All right. And can I see the imam?
◇ Is there anything wrong?
○ No. I just wanted to ask him about a fatwa.
◇ Okay, follow me. I'll show you his office.

○ *law samáḫit, wēn muṣálla -ssittēt.*
◇ *tēni bēb 3a-ššmēl. sawēni w bíb3at ḫáda yiftáḫlik ilbēb.*
○ *okē, [ᶠmerci]. w fíyi šūf[1] iššēx?*
◇ *fī šī míškli?[2]*
○ *laʔ bass báddi isʔálu 3an fátwa.*
◇ *okē, lḫaʔīni w bdíllik 3a maktábu.*

[1] قابِل *ʔēbil* **meet with**

[2] بِشو عايزْتيه؟ *bi-šū 3āyiztī?*

○ سوْري كيف مْنوصل عَ جامِع المنْصوري؟

◇ بِتْضلّكُن رايْحين بِهَيْدا الاتِّجاه، تكِنْتوا شِفْتوا محْمصْةْ الأندلُس. مدْخل الجامِع مِن بعْد هيْك بِشْوَيّ.

○ أوْكيْ، مرْسي كْتير! وفينا نْفوت[1]؟

◇ أيْه طبْعاً! لْحقوني إذا بدْكُن. أنا رايِح بِهَيْدا الاتِّجاه أصْلاً.[2]

○ مرْسي كْتير![3]

◇ وَلَوْ عيْب[4]. بسّ لازِم تِشْلحوا مِن إجْرَيْكُن[5] هونيك. فيكُن تْضلّكُن بِالكلْسات.

○ أوْكيْ عظيم. في شي تاني لازِم نعْرْفو؟

◇ السِّتّات بِالغْروب لازِم يْغطّوا شعْرُن، وممْنوع يْفوتوا إذا لابْسين شي ضيِّق أَوْ قدّ الجِسِم.

○ كِلُّن مْحضْرين حالُن للزِّيارة! مرْسي. وفينا نْصوِّر جُوّا؟

◇ فيكُن تْصوّروا صُوَر بِالسّاحة طالما ما في صلا أَوْ مَوْعِظة، بسّ بْظِنّ إنّو جُوّات[6] الجامِع ممْنوع.

○ أوْكيْ ومِنْفوت كِلّْنا عَ ذات المطْرَح[7]؟

◇ السِّتّات بيفوتوا عَ قِسْم السِّتّات هونيك عَ مَيْلِةْ اليَمين.

○ أوْكيْ، وفي مطرح يْتْوَضّوا؟

◇ أيْه، في، بسّ برّا.

○ اه أوْكيْ، يمْكِن أحْسن نْروح كِلّْنا عالحمّام قبل ما نْفوت فإذاً.

◇ أوْكيْ، عَ راحِتْكُن[8]. هلّق صِرْتوا تعْرْفوا وين تْلاقوا كِلّ شي.

○ أيْه مرْسي كْتير والله عَ لُطْفك.

◇ وَلا يْهِمّك يا عمّي[9] عيْب.

- ○ Excuse me, how can we get to Al Mansouri Mosque?
- ◇ You'll keep going in this direction until you see Al Andalous Roastery. The entrance of the mosque is just a bit after it.
- ○ Okay, thanks a lot. Is it okay to enter it?
- ◇ Oh yes. You can come along with me if you'd like. I'm going that way anyway.
- ○ Thanks a lot.
- ◇ Not at all. But you will need to take off your shoes. You can keep your socks on.
- ○ Okay, great. Anything else we should know?
- ◇ Women in the group should cover their hair, and they would not be allowed in if they're wearing anything that's form-fitting.
- ○ They're all well-prepared for this, thanks! And can we take photos inside?
- ◇ Yes, you can take as many photos as you wish in the courtyard as long as it is not during prayer time, or during a sermon. But I think it's prohibited inside the mosque itself.
- ○ Okay. Would we all go into the same area?
- ◇ The women should enter the ladies' section on the right over there.
- ○ Okay. And is there somewhere they can perform ablution?
- ◇ Yes, but it's outside.
- ○ Okay, perhaps it's better that we all go to the bathroom first, and then come back in.
- ◇ Okay, as you wish. And now you know where you can find everything.
- ○ Yes, thanks a lot for your kindness!
- ◇ Don't mention it! It's nothing!

- ○ *[sorry] kīf mnūṣal 3a jēmi3 ilmanṣūri?*
- ◇ *bitḍállkun rāyḫīn bi-háyda -lʔittijēh, ta-kíntu šíftu maḫmáṣt ilʔanadálus. mádxal iljēmi3 min ba3d hēk bi-šwáyy.*
- ○ *okē, [^{F}merci] ktīr! w fīna nfūt[1]?*

◇ *ē, ṭáb3an! lḫaʔūni íza báddkun. ána rāyiḫ bi-háyda -lʔittijēh áṣlan.*[2]
○ *[ᶠmerci] ktīr!*[3]
◇ *waláw 3ēb*[4]*. bass lēzim tišláḫu min ijráykun*[5] *hunīk. fīkun tḍállkun bi-lkalsēt.*
○ *okē 3aẓīm. fī šī tēni lēzim ná3rfu?*
◇ *-ssittēt bi-l[group] lēzim yɣáṭṭu šá3run, w mamnū3 yfūtu íza lēbsīn šī ḍáyyiʔ aw ʔadd iljísim.*
○ *kíllun mḫaḍḍrīn ḫālun la-zzyāra! [ᶠmerci]. w fīna nṣáwwir júwwa?*
◇ *fīkun tṣáwwru ṣúwar bi-ssēḫa ṭālama ma fī ṣála aw máw3iẓa, bass bẓinn ínnu juwwēt*[6] *iljēmi3 mamnū3.*
○ *okē w minfūt kíllna 3a zēt ilmáṭraḫ*[7]*?*
◇ *-ssittēt bifūtu 3a ʔísm issittēt hunīk 3a máylit ilyamīn.*
○ *okē, w fī máṭraḫ yitwáḍḍu?*
◇ *ē, fī, bass bárra.*
○ *āh okē, yímkin áḫsan nrūḫ kíllna 3a-lḫammēm ʔábil ma nfūt fa-ízan.*
◇ *okē, 3a rāḫítkun*[8]*. hálla? ṣírtu tá3rfu wēn tlēʔu kill šī.*
○ *ē, [ᶠmerci] ktīr wálla 3a lúṭfak.*
◇ *wála yhímmik ya 3ámmi*[9] *3ēb.*

[1] = نِدْخِلّو *nidxíllu*

[2] إمْشوا وَرايي، هُوِّ أساساً عَ طريقي. *ímšu warāyi, húwwi asēsan 3a ṭarīʔi.* **Follow me. It's on my way anyway.**

[3] = كِلّك ذوْق! *kíllak zōʔ!*

[4] عيْب *3ēb* is one of those words that you can use in many different contexts. It literally means 'shame.' But In this context, it means 'shame on you for thinking that you need to thank me.' Essentially, it's a 'don't mention it.' عيْب *3ēb* is also used in other contexts. For example, if children disrespect their elders, their parents may say something like يا عيْب الشّوم *ya 3ēb iššūm* **Shame on you!**

[5] تْكونوا حافْيين *tkūnu ḫāfyīn* **go barefoot**

[6] = داخِل *dēxil*

[7] = المكان *ilmakēn*

[8] = مِتِل ما بدْكُن *mítil ma báddkun*

[9] يا عمّي *ya 3ámmi* (lit. Uncle!) can be used to express genuine annoyance, as in يا عمّي خلص بقا! *ya 3ámmi, xálaş báʔa* **Enough already!** But here, it's used to feign mild offence for being thanked, something along the lines of 'Oh my God, don't worry about it!' As it is not literal or directed at the listener, it can be said to men and women.

Vocabulary

(large) mosque	*jēmi3 (jawēmi3)*	جامع (جَوامع)
(small) mosque, masjid	*másjid*	مسْجِد
minaret	*máʔzani*	مأْذنِة
dome	*ʔíbbi (ʔíbab)*	قُبّة (قُبب)
courtyard	*sēɧa*	ساحة
column	*3amūd (3wēmīd)*	عمود (عْواميد)
gate	*buwwēbi*	بُوّابِة
ticket	*tázkara (tazēkir)*	تذْكرة (تذاكِر)
to visit	*zār (yzūr)*	زار (يْزور)
shoe rack, shoe area	*maɧáll la-lʔáɧziyi/la-ljízam*	محلّ للأحْذيِة/للْجِزم
charity box	*şandūʔ işşadaʔāt*	صنْدوق الصّدقات
administration office	*máktab ilʔidāra*	مكْتب الإدارة
hijab, veil	*ɧjēb*	حْجاب
headscarf	*ţárɧa*	طرْحة
women's prayer gown	*tōb şála*	توْب صلا
skirt	*tannūra (tananīr)*	تنّورة (تنانير)

Muslim (male)	*míslim*	مِسْلِم
Muslim (female)	*misílmi*	مِسِلْمِة
ablution (ritual washing before prayer)	*wuḑūʔ*	وُضوء
to perform ablution	*twáḑḑa (yitwáḑḑa)*	تْوَضّى (يِتْوَضّى)
ablution washroom	*ɧammēm wuḑūʔ*	حمّام وُضوء
washroom, restroom	*ɧammēm*	حمّام
prayer area	*muşálla*	مُصلّى
women's section (of a mosque)	*muşálla -ssittēt*	مُصلّى السِّتّات
call to prayer	*adēn*	أدان
muezzin (person who does the call to prayer)	*muʔázzin*	مُؤذِّن
qibla (prayer direction toward Mecca)	*ʔíbli*	قِبْلِة
(ritual) prayer	*şála*	صلا
to pray (a ritual prayer)	*şálla (yşálli)*	صلّى (يْصلّي)
dawn prayer	*şalāt ilfájir* *şalāt işşúbuɧ*	صلاةْ الفجِر صلاةْ الصُّبُح
Duha prayer (voluntary morning prayer)	*şalāt iḑḑúɧa*	صلاةْ الضُّحى
noon prayer	*şalāt iḑḑúhur*	صلاةْ الضُهُر
afternoon prayer	*şalāt il3áşir*	صلاةْ العصِر

sunset prayer	*ṣalāt ilmáɣrib*	صلاةْ المغْرِب
evening prayer	*ṣalāt il3íša*	صلاةْ العِشا
prayer rug	*sijjēdit ṣála*	سِجّادِةْ صلا
people who are praying	*muṣallīn* *nēs 3am biṣállu*	مُصلّين ناس عمْ بيصلّوا
prayer, invocation	*dú3a* *dá3wi*	دُعاء دعْوِة
chanting (repetition of short prayers)	*zíkir (azkār)*	ذِكِر (أذْكار)
imam (prayer leader)	*imēm*	إمام
pulpit	*mánbar (manēbir)*	منْبر (منابِر)
sermon	*xúṭbi* *wá3ẓa* *máw3iẓa*	خُطْبِة وَعْظة مَوْعِظة
Friday	*-ljím3a*	الجِمْعة
Friday prayer	*ṣalāt iljím3a*	صلاةْ الجِمْعة
halaqa (study circle)	*ħálaʔa*	حلقة
lesson	*dáris (drūs)*	درِس (دْروس)
Quran	*qurʔān*	قُرْآن
sunna (a tradition of the Prophet)	*súnni*	سُنِّة
a religious opinion	*fátwa*	فتْوى
Ramadan	*ramaḍān*	رمضان

Taraweeh prayers (during Ramadan)	*şála -ttarāwīɧ*	صلا التّراويح
to fast	*şām (yşūm)*	صام (يْصوم)
fast(ing)	*şōm*	صوْم
breaking fast	*ifţār*	إفْطار
Eid (holiday) prayer	*şalāt il3īd*	صلاةْ العيد
holiday prayer	*şalāt il3īd*	صلاةْ العيد
funeral	*jinnēz*	جِنّاز
tomb	*ʔábir (ʔbūr)*	قبِر (قْبور)
funeral prayer	*şalāt iljinnēz*	صلاةْ الجِنّاز

Expressions

What direction do we pray in?	*bi-áyy ittijēh ilʔíbli?*	بِأيّ اِتِّجاه القِبْلِة؟
How much time is left until the midday prayer?	*ʔaddē ba3d fī wáʔit la-şalāt iđđúhur?*	قدّيْ بعْد في وَقِت لصلاةْ الضُّهُر؟
Where can I make an ablution?	*wēn fíyi itwáđđa?*	وِيْن فِيي إتْوَضّى؟
Where is the women's prayer section?	*wēn muşálla -ssittēt?* *wēn muşálla -nniswēn?*	وِيْن مُصلّى السِّتّات؟ وِيْن مُصلّى النِّسْوان؟
I'd like [to borrow] an abaya, please.	*báddi ist3īr 3abēyi, [please].*	بدّي إسْتْعير عبايِة پْليز.

◇

The sermon has just started.	*bá3da/hállaʔ mbállši -lwá3ẓa/-lmáw3iẓa.*	بعْدا/هلّق مْبلّشِة الوَعْظة/الموْعِظة.
There is some maintenance going on inside the mosque.	*fī tarmīmēt hállaʔ bi-ljēmi3.*	في ترْميمات هلّق بِالجامِع.
There are copies of the Quran and books in the library over there.	*fī maṣāḥif w kútub bi-lmáktabi hunīk.*	في مصاحِف وكُتُب بِالمكْتبِة هونيك.
Charity boxes are next to the gate on your way out.	*ṣanādīʔ iṣṣadaʔāt ḥadd ilbēb ínta w fēlil.*	صناديق الصّدقات حدّ الباب إنْتَ وفالِل.
There is a marriage ceremony after the evening prayer.	*fī kátb ktēb ba3d ṣalāt il3íša.*	في كتْب كْتاب بعْد صلاةْ العِشا.
Take an abaya to put on.	*xídi 3abēyi -lbisíya.*	خِدي عبايِة لِبْسِيا.
Women are on the upper floor.	*-ssittēt (inniswēn) bi-ṭṭābiʔ -lli fōʔ.*	السِّتّات (النِّسْوان) بِالطّابِق اللي فوْق.
There is a room for children upstairs.	*fī ūḍa la-liwlēd fōʔ.*	في أوضة للِوْلاد فوْق.

At a Church بِالكْنيسِة

While everyone is welcome at a كْنيسِة *knīsi* **church** in Lebanon, there are a few things to keep in mind. Firstly, if you're visiting a church in a village or a small town for the first time, expect people to look you up and down. They're not trying to be disrespectful, but small churches or churches in small towns rarely have newcomers, so you'd be a novelty to them. Secondly, please plan to dress modestly and respectfully. While some parishes are more liberal than others, it is better to err on the side of caution. And, while there are no particular rules as to what exactly to wear when you visit a church, it is expected that you not show too much skin. You're not expected to wear a headscarf or long sleeves, but you also shouldn't be wearing short skirts or dresses, shorts, or strapless or low-cut tops. Many people dress up for church, especially if it's Sunday mass. People especially like to dress up their children, more than they dress up themselves! Lastly, it's important to keep in mind that you can only receive communion in a Catholic church if you are baptized. In general, just observe the same etiquette you would in any other place of worship. Be respectful of others and as quiet as possible, unless you're participating in church hymns or chants; do not use your cellphone; and don't eat inside the church. Photography is acceptable unless otherwise noted, and as long as a service is not in progress.

Looking for a Church

○ لَوْ سمحْتي، كْنيسِةْ مار شرْبِل ويْن؟[1]

◇ إذا بِتْضلِّك سايْقة دِغْري، بِتْشوفي سْتانْد حِلو عَ يمَينِك. بِتْضلِّك رايْحة. ما تْروحي لا يمَين وَلا شْمال. بِتْشوفي الكْنيسِة هونيك عَ آخِر الطّريق.

○ تمام، مرسي.

◇ بسّ خلّي بِبالِك إنّو مع إنّو ما في قاعْدِة مكْتوبِة عن اللِّبِس، ما بيحبّذوا إنّو تْفوتي بِتنّورة قصيرِة.

○ قِلِت هيْك أنا، فجِبِت معي بنْطلوْن بِلِبْسو قبِل ما فوت. مرْسي كْتير!

○ Excuse me, where is the St. Charbel church?

◇ If you keep driving straight, you'll see a sweets kiosk on your right-hand side. Keep going, don't make any turns, and you'll see it there at the end of the road.

○ Excellent - thank you!

◇ But bear in mind that, although there's no written rule about dress code, it is frowned upon if you enter wearing a short skirt.

○ I figured, so I brought a pair of pants I'll slip on. Thanks so much!

○ *law samáħti, knīsit mār šárbil wēn?*[1]

◇ *íza bitḍállik sēyʔa díɣri, bitšūfi [stand] ħílu 3a yamīnik. bitḍállik rāyħa. ma trūħi la yamīn wála šmēl. bitšūfi liknīsi hunīk 3a ēxir iṭṭarīʔ.*

○ *tamēm, [Fmerci].*

◇ *bass xálli bi-bēlik ínnu ma3 ínnu ma fī ʔā3di maktūbi 3an illíbis, ma biħábbzu ínnu tfūti bi-tannūra ʔaṣīri.*

○ *ʔílit hēk ána, fa-jíbit má3i banṭalōn bilíbsu ʔábil ma fūt. [Fmerci] ktīr!*

1 عفْواً، كيف فِيي أوصل عَ... *3áfwan, kīf fíyi ūṣal 3a...* **Excuse me, how can I get to...?**

2 كِرْمال هيْك جِبْت معي تْياب مِحْتِشْمِة. *kirmēl hēk jibt má3i tyēb miḫtíšmi.* **That's why I brought some modest clothes with me.**

2

Dressing appropriately

◇ عفْواً، ما فيكي تْفوتي بِهَوْدي التّْياب. كْتير مْظلّطين للِكْنيسِة. حُطّي هَيْدا الشّال عَ كْتافِك.[1]

○ معي شال بِالسِّيّارة. رح روح جيبو وإرْجع.

◇ كْتير مْنيح. طالما مْغطّايِة، ما بيهِمّْني أيّا شال بْتِسْتعْمْلي.[2]

○ أوْكي، مرْسي كْتير.

◇ Excuse me, you can't enter wearing that outfit. It's too revealing for church. Put this scarf on your shoulders.

○ I have a scarf in the car. I'll go back and get it.

◇ Very well, then. As long as you're covered, I don't care which scarf you use.

○ Okay, thank you.

◇ *3áfwan, ma fīki tfūti bi-háwdi -ttyēb. ktīr mẓallaṭīn la-liknīsi. ḫúṭṭi háyda -ššēl 3a ktēfik.*[1]

○ *má3i šēl bi-ssiyyāra. raḫ rūḫ jību w írja3.*

◇ *ktīr mnīḫ. ṭālama mɣaṭṭāyi, ma bihímmni áyya šēl btistá3mli.*[2]

○ *okē, [ᶠmerci] ktīr.*

1 غطّي كْتافِك. *ɣáṭṭi ktēfik.* **Cover your shoulders.**

2 ما بْتِفْرُق. المُهِم تْغطّي كْتافِك. *ma btífru?. -lmuhímm tɣáṭṭi ktēfik.* **It doesn't matter. What's important is that you cover your shoulders.**

3

Asking permission

o لَوْ سمحْتي، بدّي شوف إذا يَلّي مِش مسيحية فِيُن يْفوتوا عالِكْنيسِة؟

◇ أهْلا وسهْلا بِالكِلّ عالِكْنيسِة.[1] بسّ ما فيك تِتْناوَل إلّا إذا كِنِت معْمد كاتوْليك.

o اه أوْكي، فْهِمِت علَيْكي. وفينا ناخُد صُوَر[2]؟

◇ فيك تْصوِّر طالما ما في قِدّاس.

o Excuse me, I'm wondering if non-Christians are allowed in the church?

◇ Everyone is welcome to the church. But you can't take communion unless you're a baptized Catholic.

o Oh okay, I see. And, are we allowed to take pictures?

◇ You can take pictures as long as mass is not in session.

o *law samáħti, báddi šūf íza yálli miš masīħíyyi fíyun yfūtu 3a-liknīsi?*

◇ *áhla w sáhla bi-lkíll 3a-liknīsi.*[1] *bass ma fīk titnēwal ílla íza kínit má3mad kētōlīk.*

o *āh okē, fhímit 3láyki. w fīna nēxud şúwar*[2]*?*

◇ *fīk tşáwwir ţālama ma fī ʔiddēs.*

[1] = مُرحّب بِالكِلّ عالكْنيسِة *muráħħab bi-lkíll 3a-liknīsi.*

[2] = نِتْصوّر *nitşáwwar*

Popular churches among Lebanese and tourists include St. Charbel, Our Lady of Lebanon, and the Lady of Bechawate.

4

Following rules

◇ دْمْوازيْل، ما فيكي تْفوتي مع الأكِل هيْك.[1]

○ شو بعْمِل فيِنْ؟ ما بدّي كِبّنْ.

◇ مِش ضروري تْكِبّينْ، بسّ ما فيكي تْفوتي عم تاكْلي بِقلِب الكْنيسِة. غطّينْ عْمِلي معْروف وحُطّينْ بِجزْدانِك.

○ طيِّب، أوْكي. مرْسي.

◇ مِش مشْكل. الله يِسْتقْبِل مِنِّك.

◇ Miss, you're not allowed to go in with the food.

○ What do I do with it? I don't want to throw it out!

◇ You don't need to throw it out, but you can't be eating it inside the church. Please cover it and put it in your purse.

○ Okay, fine. Thank you.

◇ No problem. May the Lord hear and answer your prayers.

◇ *[Fdemoiselle], ma fīki tfūti ma3 ilʔákil hēk.*[1]

○ *šū bá3mil fíyun? ma báddi kíbbun.*

◇ *miš ḍarūri tkíbbiyun, bass ma fīki tfūti 3am tēkli bi-ʔálib liknīsi. ɣaṭṭíyun 3míli ma3rūf w ḫuṭṭíyun bi-jizdēnik.*

○ *ṭáyyib, okē. [Fmerci].*

◇ *miš máškal. álla yistáʔbil mínnik.*

[1] الأكِل مِش مسْموح جُوّا. *-lʔákil miš masmūḫ gúwwa.* **Food isn't allowed inside.**

5

Asking about Mass (1)

○ عفوًا، في شي قِدّاسات بِالإنْجْليزي اليوْم؟

◇ لأ لِلأسف[1]، القِدّاسات بسّ بِالعربي.

○ طيِّب بيكون في غيرْ يوْم؟

◇ لأ ما في قِدّاسات بِالإنْجْليزي بِهَيْدي الرّعية. صراحة ما بعْرِف إذا غيرْ رعايا بيقدْمُوْن. بسّ القِدّاس كْتير قريب مْن القِدّاسات الكاتوْليك برّا، فمفْروض يْكون فيكي تْتابْعي معُن بِغالبيةْ الإشْيا.[2]

○ Excuse me, are there masses in English today?

◇ No, unfortunately, masses are only in Arabic.

○ Are they offered on a different day?

◇ No, English masses are not offered in this parish. To be honest, I don't know of any other churches that offer them, either. But, the proceedings of the mass are very similar to the those of a catholic mass abroad; so, you should be able to follow along, more or less.

○ *3áfwan, fī šī ʔiddēsēt bi-lʔinglīzi -lyōm?*

◇ *laʔ, li-lʔásaf*[1]*, -lʔiddēsēt bass bi-l3árabi.*

○ *ṭáyyib bikūn fī ɣēr yōm?*

◇ *laʔ ma fī ʔiddēsēt bi-lʔinglīzi bi-háydi -rra3íyyi. ṣarāḥa ma bá3rif íza ɣēr ra3āya bi-ʔaddmúwun. bass ilʔiddēs ktīr ʔarīb mn ilʔiddēsēt ilkatolīk bárra, fa-mafrūḍ ykūn fīki ttēb3i má3un bi-ɣēlibíyyit ilʔíšya.*[2]

[1] = لأ بِعْتِذِر مِنِّك. *laʔ, bi3tízir mínnik.*

[2] ما عِندي فِكْرة. *ma 3índi fíkra.* **I have no idea.**

6

Asking about mass (2)

○ عفْواً، أيّا ساعة القِدّاس؟

◇ القِدّاس بيبلِّش عالخمْسِة ونُصّ.

○ عظيم. وقدّيْ بيضلّ؟[1]

◇ إجْمالاً ساعة، بسّ بِفْتِكِر اليوْم القِدّاس الأرْبْعين لمرا مْن الرّعية، يَعْني بْيِبْقوا الكِلّ مِن بعْد القِدّاس تَيْصلّوا صلى عن راحِةْ نفْسا، بْيرِْجعوا بيروحوا الكِلّ عَ صالةْ الرّعية لِلقْمِةْ الرّحْمِة[2] بِتْقدِّما عَيْلِةْ الفقيدِة وبْيِتْقبّلوا التّعازي.

○ اه أوف. الله يِرْحما.

◇ مرْسي، تْعيشي وتِترْحّمي.

○ Excuse me, what time is mass?

◇ The next service starts at 5:30pm.

○ Awesome! And how long is it?

◇ It's usually an hour, but I think today is the 40-day memorial of a late parishioner, which means worshippers stay after for a special prayer for her soul, followed by a bite at the church hall, offered by the family of the deceased to everyone who'd like to pay them condolences.

○ Oh... May her soul rest in peace.

◇ Thank you. May you live and pray for her soul.

○ *3áfwan, áyya sē3a -lʔiddēs?*

◇ *-lʔiddēs bibálliš 3a-lxámsi w nuṣṣ.*

○ *3aẓīm. w ʔaddē biḍáll?*[1]

◇ *ijmēlan sē3a, bass bíftikir ilyōm ilʔiddēs ilʔarb3īn la-mára mn irra3íyyi, yá3ni byíbʔu -lkill min ba3d ilʔiddēs ta-yṣállu ṣála 3an rāḫit náfsa, byírja3u birūḫu -lkill 3a ṣalāt irra3íyyi la-líʔmit irráḫmi*[2] *bitʔáddima 3áylit -lfaʔīdi w byitʔábbalu -tta3ēzi.*

○ *āh ūf. álla yirḫáma.*

◇ [ᶠmerci], t3īši w titráɧɧami.

[1] بيطوِّل كْتير؟ *biţáwwil ktīr.* **Does it take a long time?**

[2] لِقْمِةْ الرّحْمِة *líʔmit irráɧmi* (lit. a bite of mercy) is, essentially, the meal that the family of the deceased serves at the church hall to the parishioners and other friends and family who come to pay their condolences.

Extended Dialogue

○ عفْواً، كيف فينا نوصل عَ سيّْدِةْ لِبْنان؟

◇ بْتْضلِّك رايْحة بِهَيْدا الاِتِّجاه، تْشوفي آرْمة عْلَيا حريصة، ساعِتا بْتِطْلعي بِالطّلْعة اللي حدّا. وبِتْضلِّك رايْحة دِغْري تتوصلي عالكْنيسِة.

○ أوْكيْ مرْسي! وفِيْن يَلّي منُّن مسيحية يْفوتوا؟

◇ أيْه أكيد! السُّواح مِن ويْن ما كان بْيِجوا. حتّى اللِّبْنانية مِن كلّ الدِّيانات بيزوروا الكْنيسِة، مِش بسّ لِأنّو حِلْوِة، بسّ كمان لِأنّو عِنْدا معاني روحية للبْنان.

○ حِلو كْتير. مرْسي عالمعْلومات!

◇ وَلا يْهِمّك. بسّ انْتِبْهي، الأرْجح ما يْخلّوكي تْفوتي بِفِسْطان قصير.

○ مرْسي لِأنّو قِلْتيلي! هلّق باخُد شي مِن رْفيقْتي وبْغيرّ قبِل ما فوت.

◇ مْنيح. ما بيحدِّدوا عالمظْبوط شو مسْموح وشو ممْنوع، بسّ في أرْمات بْيِطْلُبو مْن الزُّوار يْكونوا مِحْتِشْمين. فأحْسن تْروحي عالمضْمون!

○ مرْسي كْتير! في شي تاني لازِم أعْرْفو؟

◇ في ناس بيوَقْفوا هونيك حدّ الأرْمة وبْياخْدوا التِّلفريك لفوْق وبْيِرْجعوا بْيِنْزلوا فيه لهوْن. حِلو المِشْوار، بِتْشوفي جونْيِة والبحِر.

o أوْكي، كْتير مْنيح. مرْسي عالنّصايِح! وفوْق، مسْموح نِطْلع عِنْد الشّخِص[1]؟

◇ أيْه! هَيْدا أحْلى جِزْء مْن الزْيارة والأكْتر شعْبية!

o حِلو. وعم قدِّر في حمّامات فوْق؟[2]

◇ أيْه وفي مطاعِم وكم سْتانْد أكِل.

o عظيم! مرْسي كْتير عَ كِلّ شي!

◇ وَلا يْهِمِّك! الله يِسْتقْبِل مِنْكُن.

o مرْسي، انْشالله يْكون نْهارِك حِلو.

◇ وإنْتي كمان.

o Excuse me, how can we get to the Lady of Lebanon?

◇ You'll keep going in this direction until you see a sign for 'Harissa,' at which point you'll go up the hill and keep going up straight and following the signs until you reach the church.

o Okay, thank you. Is it okay for non-Christians to enter it?

◇ Yes, of course. Tourists come from all over to visit. Even Lebanese people from all religions visit the church not only for its beauty and stunning views but also its spiritual significance for Lebanon.

o That's wonderful! Thank you for the information!

◇ Not at all. But keep in mind that you probably won't be allowed with a short dress.

o Thanks for letting me know! I'll borrow something from my friend and change before going in.

◇ Good. They don't exactly specify what's allowed and what isn't, but there are signs asking that visitors dress modestly. So, it's better to be on the safe side.

o Thanks a lot! Anything else we should know?

◇ Some people park by that sign over there and ride the cable cars up then back down. It's a sweet ride overlooking Jounieh and the sea.

- o Okay. Awesome! Thanks for the tip! And, up there, are we allowed to walk up to the statue?
- ◇ Yes! That's the best part of the visit and the most popular!
- o Nice! And I presume there are bathrooms up there?
- ◇ Yep, there are even restaurants and a couple of food kiosks.
- o Great! Thanks so much for everything!
- ◇ It's my pleasure. May your visit be accepted by God.
- o Thank you! Have a great day.
- ◇ You do the same.

- o *3áfwan, kīf fīna nūṣal 3a sáyydit libnēn?*
- ◇ *bitdállik rāyḫa bi-háyda -lʔittijēh, ta-tšūfi ārma 3láya ḫarīṣa, sē3íta btíṭla3i bi-ṭṭál3a -lli ḫádda. w bitdállik rāyḫa díɣri ta-tūṣali 3a-liknīsi.*
- o *okē [[F]merci]! w fíyun yálli mánnun masīḫíyyi yfūtu?*
- ◇ *ē, akīd! issuwēḫ min wēn ma kēn byíju. ḫátta -llibnēníyyi min kill iddiyēnēt bizūru liknīsi, miš bass li-ánnu ḫílwi, bass kamēn li-ánnu 3índa ma3ēni rūḫíyyi la-libnēn.*
- o *ḫílu ktīr. [[F]merci] 3a-lma3lūmēt!*
- ◇ *wála yhímmik. bass ntíbhi, -lʔárjaḫ ma yxallūki tfūti bi-fisṭān ʔaṣīr.*
- o *[[F]merci] li-ánnu ʔiltīli! hállaʔ bēxud šī min rfīʔti w byáyyir ʔábil ma fūt.*
- ◇ *mnīḫ. ma biḫádiddu 3a-lmaẓbūṭ šū masmūḫ w šū mamnū3, bass fī armēt byíṭlubu mn izzuwār ykūnu miḫtišmīn. fa-áḫsan trūḫi 3a-lmaḍmūn!*
- o *[[F]merci] ktīr! fī šī tēni lēzim á3rfu?*
- ◇ *fī nēs biwáʔʔfu hunīk ḫadd ilʔárma w byēxdu -t[[F]téléphérique] la-fōʔ w byirjá3u byínzalu fī la-hōn. ḫílu -lmišwār, bitšūfi jūnyi w ilbáḫir.*
- o *okē, ktīr mnīḫ. [[F]merci] 3a-nnaṣāyiḫ! w fōʔ, masmūḫ níṭla3 3ind iššáxiṣ[1]?*
- ◇ *ē,! háyda áḫla jizʔ mn izzyāra w ilʔáktar ša3bíyyi!*
- o *ḫílu. w 3am ʔáddir fī ḫammēmēt fōʔ?[2]*
- ◇ *ē, w fī maṭā3im w kam [stand] ákil.*
- o *3aẓīm! [[F]merci] ktīr 3a kill šī!*
- ◇ *wála yhímmik! álla yistáʔbil mínkun.*

○ [Fmerci], nšálla ykūn nhārik ḫílu.
◇ w ínti kamēn.

[1] = التِّمْثال *ittimsēl*

[2] قَوْلك في حمّامات فوْق؟ *ʔáwlak fī ḫammēmēt fōʔ?* **Do you think there are restrooms upstairs?**

Vocabulary

church	*knīsi (kanēyis)*	كْنيسِة (كنايِس)
priest	*xūri (xawārni)* *abūna*	خوري (خَوارْنِة) أبونا
nun	*rāhbi* *[Fma sœur]*	راهْبِة ما سور
mass	*ʔiddēs*	قِدّاس
service during mass (on the altar)	*xídmit ilʔiddēs*	خِدْمِةْ القِدّاس
funeral	*dáfin*	دفِن
cemetary	*máʔbara (maʔābir)*	مقْبرة (مقابِر)
coffin	*tēbūt*	تابوت
wedding	*3íris*	عِرِس
parish	*ra3íyyi*	رعية
parishioners	*sukkēn irra3íyyi*	سُكّان الرّعية
chanting, hymn-singing	*tartīl (tarātīl)*	ترْتيل (تراتيل)
prayer	*ṣála*	صلا
celebratory masses	*ʔiddēs iḫtifēli*	قِدّاس اِحْتِفالي

patriarch	*báṭrak*	بطْرك
communion	*ʔirbēn/ ʔirbēni (ʔarābīn)* *biršāni*	قِرْبان/قِرْبانِة (قرابين) بِرْشانِة
first communion	*áwwal ʔirbēni*	أوّل قِرْبانِة
taking communion	*munēwali*	مْناوَلِة
monastery, convent	*dēr (adyíra)*	ديْر (أدْيْرة)
confession	*i3tirāf*	اِعْتِراف
Christmas	*(3īd) ilmīlād*	(عيد) الميلاد
Good Friday	*-ljím3a -l3aẓīmi*	الجِمْعة العظيمِة
Easter	*-lfíṣiḫ* *[^FPâques]*	الفِصِح پاك
The Holy Spirit	*-rrūḫ ilʔídis*	الرّوح القِدِس
Jesus Christ	*yasū3 ilmasīḫ*	يَسوع المسيح
to take communion	*tnēwal (yitnēwal)*	تْناوَل (يِتْناوَل)
religion	*dīn (adyēn)*	دين (أدْيان)
Maronite (sect)	*mārūni (mwārni)*	ماروني (مْوارْنِة)
Orthodox	*[^Forthodoxe]*	أُرْتوْدُكْس
Roman Catholic	*rūm kātōlīk*	روم كاتوْليك
The Pope	*-lbāba (rōma)*	البابا (روْما)
soloist	*[solo]*	سوْلوْ
deacon	*šammēs (šamēmse)*	شمّاس (شمامْسِة)
donation basket, offering plate	*ṣaníyyi*	صنية

sect	*ţāyfi*	طايْفِة
baptism	*3mēdi*	عْمادِة
chorus, choir	*[^F chorale]* *jáwʔa*	كوْرال جَوْقة
sermon	*wá3ẓa* *máw3iẓa*	وَعْظة، مَوْعِظة

Expressions

What time is mass today?	*áyya sē3a ilʔiddēs ilyōm?*	أيّا ساعة القِدّاس اليوْم؟
Are there masses today?	*fī ʔiddēsēt ilyōm?*	في قِدّاسات اليوْم؟
Who's the priest in this parish?	*mīn ilxūri bi-háydi -rra3íyyi?*	مين الخوري بِهَيْدي الرّعية؟
Is there a mass in English?	*fī šī ʔiddēs bi-lʔinglīzi?*	في شي قِدّاس بِالإنْجْليزي؟
Where are the mass-books?	*wēn kútub ilʔiddēs?*	ويْن كُتُب القِدّاس؟
Will there be confessions available?	*fī šī i3tirāfēt?* *fī majēl ni3tírif?*	في شي اِعْتِرافات؟ في مجال نِعْترِف؟

Dealing with the Police حكي مع الدّرك

الشُّرْطة *-ššúrṭa* or الدّرك *-ddárak* **the police** in Lebanon have come a long way in recent years in terms of doing their job and apprehending those who have broken the law. Still, they have a long way to go! That is not to discourage you from seeking help from the police when things go wrong or you need to report a robbery, for example. It is, however, to warn you against relying too much on the police and expecting that matters will be resolved just because you have filed a police report. Matters of sexual or verbal harassment are, unfortunately, still not being taken as seriously as they should be. As such, it is probably best to keep the your embassy's number handy, in the event that the police doesn't come through for you. The U.S. Embassy in Beirut accepts emergency calls 24 hours a day, seven days a week. You can reach them at 04-543600 from within Lebanon, according to their website, as of press time.

Reporting a theft

o بدّي بلّغ عن سِرْقة لَوْ سمحِت.

◇ شو نْسرق عالمظْبوط؟

o شنْطْتي. كانِت بِالتّاكْسي اللي أخدْناه[1] مْن المطار.

◇ معِك رقْم التّاكْسي؟[2]

o أيْه هِيّاه هوْن.

o I want to report a theft, please.

◇ What was stolen exactly?

o My suitcase. It was in the taxi that I took from the airport.

◇ Well, do you have the taxi number?

o Yes, here it is.

o *báddi bálliɣ 3an sírʔa, law samáḩit.*

◇ *šū nsáraʔ 3a-lmaẓbūṭ?*

o *šánṭti. kēnit bi-ttáksi -lli axadnē[1] mn ilmaṭār.*

◇ *má3ik ráʔm ittáksi?[2]*

o *ē, hiyyē hōn.*

[1] جابْني *jēbni* **took me**

[2] أخدْتي رقْمو؟ *axádti ráʔmu?* **Did you get his [license plate] number?**

2

Reporting a Crime

o مدام، عْطيتي مِفْتاح بَيْتِك لحدا؟

◇ ما حدا عِنْدو مْفاتيح بَيْتي إلّا صاحِب الملِك اللي سْتأْجرت مِنّو.

o أوْكي، معْقول تْكوني تركْتي شي باب البيْت مفْتوح بسّ فلّيْتي؟

◇ لأ أبداً، ورْجِعِت عَ هَيْدا المنْظر، مِتِل منّك[1] شايِف، والمصاري مسْروقة.

◇ Ma'am, have you given your house key to anyone?

o No one has the keys except the landlord I rented from.

◇ Okay, did you leave the door open when you left?

o No, not at all. I came back to find this scene, as you can see, and the money stolen.

o *[Fmadame], 3ṭīti miftēḫ báytik la-ḫáda?*

◇ *ma ḫáda 3índu mfētīḫ báyti ílla ṣāḫib ilmílik -lli sta?járit mínnu.*

o *okē, ma3?ūl tkūni tarákti šī bēb ilbēt maftūḫ bass falláyti?*

◇ *la? ábadan, w rjí3it 3a háyda -lmánẓar, mítil mánnak[1] šēyif, w ilmaṣāri masrū?a.*

[1] مَنّك *mánnak* can mean **you are not**. However, here, it is another way of saying colloquially ما إنْتَ *ma ínta*. So مِتِل مَنِّك شايْفِة *mítil mánnik šāyfi* means مِتِل ما إنْتي شايْفِة *mítil ma ínti šāyfi* **as you see**.

3

Dealing with a ransom

o أنا بِشْتِغِل بِالسّفارة، واللاپْتوْپ عْليْه ملفّات كْتير مْهِمّة.

◇ تّصلوا فيكي يَلّي سرقوا مِنّك؟

o عم يِطِلْبوا فِدْية ٢٠,٠٠٠ دوْلار تَيْرِدّولي ياه.

◇ طيِّب، خلّينا نْحوِّل القضية عَ مكْتب مكافحِةْ الجرايِم المعْلوماتيّةْ، وهِنِّ بيِهْتمّوا بِكِلّ شي.

o I work at the embassy, and my laptop contains extremely important documents.

◇ And have those who stole it from you contacted you?

o They're asking for a $20,000 ransom to return it.

◇ Okay, let's transfer this case to the Cybercrime Combatting Bureau, and they will handle everything.

o *ána bištíɣil bi-ssafāra, w il[laptop] 3lē malaffēt ktīr mhímmi.*

◇ *ttáṣalu fīki yálli sáraʔu mínnik?*

o *3am yiṭilbu fídyi 3išrīn alf dólar ta-yriddūli yēh.*

◇ *ṭáyyib, xallīna nḫáwwil ilʔaḍíyyi 3a máktab mukēfaḫit -ljarāyim ilma3lūmētíyyi, w hínni byihtámmu bi-kíll šī.*

○ فِيي أعْرِف ليْه أنا هوْن؟[1]

◇ مُتّهَم[2] بِتِبْييض أمْوال، وجِبْناك لهوْن تنْحقِّق معك.

○ لأ، حضْرِةْ الظّابِط. هَيْدي القُصّة ما فِيا تْكون أبْعد مْن الحقيقة.[3] بدّي إتِّصِل بمُحامِيّ.

○ Can I know why I'm here?

◇ You're accused of money laundering, and you're here so we can question you.

○ No, Officer. This cannot be further from the truth. I need to call my lawyer.

○ *fíyi á3rif lē ána hōn?*[1]

◇ *muttáham*[2] *bi-tibyīḑ amwēl, w jibnēk la-hōn tanħáʔʔiʔ má3ak.*

○ *laʔ, ħáḑrit iḑḑābiţ. háydi -lʔúşşa ma fíya tkūn áb3ad mn ilħaʔīʔa.*[3] *báddi ittíşil bi-muħāmíyyi.*

[1] فِيي أعْرِف شو تِهِمْتي؟ *fíyi á3rif šū tihímti?* **Can I know what I'm being accused of?**

[2] مُشْتبه *muštábah* **suspected**

[3] خياليِّة *xayēlíyyi* **fiction, imaginary**; باطْلِة *bāţli* **false, unfounded**; إفْتِراء *iftirāʔ* **slander**

5

TRAFFIC FINE

◇ ما كِنْت عارْفِة إنّو ممْنوع وَقِّف[1] هوْن.
o وْراقِك وضبِط خمْسين ألْف.[2]
◇ لِلأسف، ضيّعِت دفْتري السّواقة.
o هَيْدا ضبِط تاني. عْطيني دفْتر السِّيّارة عْمِلي معْروف وتْفضّلي طْلعي مْن السِّيّارة.

◇ I didn't know parking is not allowed here.
o Your papers and a 50,000 L.L. fine.
◇ I have unfortunately lost my driver's license.
o That's another fine. Give me the car registration, please, and step out of the vehicle.

◇ *ma kínt 3ārfi ínnu mamnū3 wáʔʔif[1] hōn.*
o *wrāʔik w ḍābiṭ xamsīn alf.[2]*
◇ *li-lʔásaf, ḍayyá3it dáftari -sswēʔa.*
o *háyda ḍābiṭ tēni. 3ṭīni dáftar issiyyāra 3míli ma3rūf w tfáḍḍali ṭlá3i mn issiyyāra.*

[1] = صِفّ *ṣiff*

[2] رح أعْطيكي ظبِط مْخالفِة. *raḥ a3ṭīki ẓábiṭ mxēlafi.* **I'm going to give you a ticket.**

6

Traffic accident

○ ما تْواخِذْني حضْرِةْ الضّابِط، بسّ هُوِّ فاتِ فِيي[1] مِن وَرا. يَعْني الحقّ عْليْه.

◇ بسّ إنْتي كمان وَقّفْتي فجْأة.

○ إنْتَ شِفِت بِعَيْنيْك المرا اللي كانِت عم تِقْطع الطّريق. لَوْ ما وَقّفِت، كِنِت فِتِت فِيا[2].

◇ أوْكي. بِتْحِبّوا تْحِلّوا حُبِّيّاً وِلّا بدْكُن تِفْتحوا محْضر؟

○ Pardon me, officer, he is the one who crashed into me from behind. Therefore, he's in the wrong.

◇ But you stopped all of a sudden, too.

○ You saw yourself the lady who crossed in front of me. If I hadn't stopped, I would have run her over.

◇ Okay, would you like to end this dispute in a friendly manner or shall we make a report?

○ *ma twēxízni ḫádrit iḏḏābiṭ, bass húwwi fēt fíyi[1] min wára. yá3ni -lḫa?? 3lē.*

◇ *bass ínti kamēn wa??áfti fáj?a.*

○ *ínta šíft b-3aynēk ilmára -lli kēnit 3am tí?ṭa3 iṭṭarī?. law ma wa??áfit, kínit fítit fíya[2].*

◇ *okē. bitḫíbbu tḫílluwa ḫubbíyyan wílla báddkun tíftaḫu máḫḏar?*

[1] = ضرب فِيي *ḏárab fíyi*

[2] = كِنِت هرسْتا *kínit harásta*

○ لَوْ سمحِت، بدّي بلِّغ عن ڤانْدوز[1] بمِحلّ.

◇ شو عِمْلِتْلِك؟

○ سرقِت مصاري مِن شنْطتي.

◇ قدّيْ؟[2]

○ خمْسْتلاف دوْلار.

◇ أوْكيْ، خلّينا نْروح عالمخْفر لكان.[3]

○ أوْكيْ، ويْن أقْرب مرْكز؟

◇ لْحقيني، مْنِفْتح محْضر. معِك پاسْپوْرِك؟

○ أيه، معي پاسْپوْري.

◇ ووِيْن هَيْدا المحلّ عالمظْبوط؟

○ بِجْبيْل، بِالسّوق العتيق. هَيْدا كيس مْن المحلّ. أنا مِتْأكْدِة إنّو هِيِّ اللي سرقِتْن.

◇ فيكي تْقوليلي شو صار عالمظْبوط؟

○ أوْكيْ، كِنْت عم بِحْكي مع تْنيْن بيّاعين. زلمِة، ووِحْدِة عَيْنيّا خُضُر وشعْرا أسْوَد.

◇ أوْكيْ، وبعْديْن؟[4]

○ فجْأة، المرا بْتِخْتِفي، أنا وعم شارِع الشّبّ عالسِّعر. بعْد شْوَيّ، بِتْفوت وِحْدِة كأنّا سايْحة، بسّ كانِت ذات شكْل الڤانْدوز اللي كان بعْدا مِخْفية بسّ مْغيْرِة تْيابا.

◇ يَلّي عيْنيّا خُضُر وشعْرا أسْوَد؟

○ أيه مظْبوط، هِيّاها. كانِت لابْسِة كأنّا سايْحة، وحسّيْت كأنّو شي عم يِتْحرّك بِجِزْداني، بِذات الوَقِت اللي بلّش فيه هيداك البيّاع يْفرْجيني تْياب تانْيِة تَيِلْهيني.

◇ شاكّة إنّو عم يِشْتِغْلوا سَوا؟
o مِش شاكّة، متْأكّدِة، لِأنّو أوّل ما بلّش يِلْهيني البيّاع، هَيْديك أخدِت المصاري وفلّت.
◇ عَ كِلّ الأحْوال، رح تْعبّي محْضر تْصرْحي عن كِلّ هالإشْيا. حُطّي كِلّ التّفاصيل، وحدّدي ويْن المحلّ عالمظْبوط.

o Excuse me, I want to report a salesperson in a shop.
◇ What did she do to you?
o She stole money out of my bag.
◇ How much?
o $5,000.
◇ Okay, let's go to the police station then.
o All right. Where is the nearest police station?
◇ Follow me. we'll file a police report. Do you have your passport on you?
o Yes, I have my passport.
◇ And where is this shop exactly?
o In Jbeil, in the Old Souk. Here's the plastic bag from the shop. I'm sure she's the one who stole it.
◇ Can you tell me what happened exactly?
o I was talking to two salespeople; a man, and a woman with green eyes and black hair
◇ Okay, and then?
o All of the sudden, the woman disappeared while I was haggling with the other guy. Then, a few moments later, a woman came in as if she were a tourist, but she had the same look as the saleswoman who left earlier, but she had changed his clothes.
◇ The one with green eyes and black hair?
o Exactly, that one. She was dressed like a tourist, and I felt some movement in my bag, while the salesman started to show me other stuff to distract me.
◇ Do you suspect they're together?

- I don't suspect; I'm certain of it. Because the moment the salesman started distracting me, the other took the money and vanished.
- ◇ In any case, you will file a report stating all this. Write out all the details, and describe to the officer the location of the shop.

- *law samáħit, báddi bálliɣ 3an [ᶠvendeuse]*[1] *bi-maħáll.*
- ◇ *šū 3imlítlik?*
- *sáraʔit maṣāri min šánṭti.*
- ◇ *ʔaddēʔ?*[2]
- *xamstalēf dólar.*
- ◇ *okē, xallīna nrūħ 3a-lmáxfar lakēn.*[3]
- *okē, wēn áʔrab márkaz?*
- ◇ *lħaʔīni, mníftaħ máħḍar. má3ik paspōrik?*
- *ē, má3i paspōri.*
- ◇ *w wēn háyda -lmaħáll 3a-lmaẓbūṭ?*
- *bi-jbēl, bi-ssūʔ il3atīʔ. háyda kīs mn ilmaħáll. ána mitʔákkdi ínnu híyyi -lli saraʔítun.*
- ◇ *fīki tʔūlīli šū ṣār 3a-lmaẓbūṭ?*
- *okē, kínt 3am bíħki ma3 tnēn bayyē3īn. zálami, w wíħdi 3aynáyya xúḍur w šá3ra áswad.*
- ◇ *okē, w ba3dēn?*[4]
- *fájʔa, -lmára btixtífi, ána w 3am šēri3 iššább 3a-ssí3ir. ba3d šwayy, bitfūt wíħdi ka-ánna sēyħa, bass kēnit zēt šakl il[ᶠvendeuse] -lli kēn bá3da mixfíyyi bass mɣáyyra tyēba.*
- ◇ *yálli 3aynáyya xúḍur w šá3ra áswad?*
- *ē, maẓbūṭ, hiyyēha. kēnit lēbsi ka-ánna sēyħa, w ħassēt ka-ánnu šī 3am yitħárrak bi-jizdēni, bi-zēt ilwáʔit -lli bállaš fī hidēk ilbayyē3 yfarjīni tyēb tēnyi ta-yilhīni.*
- ◇ *šēkki ínnu 3am yištíɣlu sáwa?*
- *miš šēkki, mitʔákkdi, li-ánnu áwwal ma bállaš yilhīni -lbayyē3, haydīk áxadit ilmaṣāri w fállit.*
- ◇ *3a kill ilʔaħwēl, raħ t3ábbi máħḍar tṣárrħi 3an kill ha-lʔíšya. ħúṭṭi kill ittafāṣīl, w ħaddídi wēn ilmaħáll 3a-lmaẓbūṭ.*

[1] = بيّاعة *bayyē3a*

[2] = قدّيْ المبْلغ؟ *ʔaddē -lmáblaɣ?*

3 خلّينا نروح نِفْتح محْضر. *xallīna nrūђ níftaђ máђḑar.* **Let's go file a report.**

4 كمّْلي *kámmli* = كفّيلي *kaffīli* **Continue!, Go on!**

Vocabulary

police station	*máxfar*	مخْفر
checkpoint	*ђājiz*	حاجِز
police officer	*dáraki*	دركي
soldier	*3áskari*	عسْكري
to report	*bállaɣ (ybálliɣ)*	بلّغ (يْبلِّغ)
report	*máђḑar* *balēɣ*	محْضر بلاغ
complaint	*šákwa*	شكْوى
to accuse of	*ttáham (yítthim) bi-*	تّهم (يِتّْهِم) بِـ
suspect; accused	*muttáham*	مُتّهم
criminal	*míjrim*	مِجْرِم
suspected	*muštábah fī*	مُشْتبَه فيه
to steal; to rob	*sáraʔ (yísruʔ)*	سرق (يِسْرُق)
theft	*sírʔa*	سِرْقة
thief	*ђarāmi*	حرامي
pickpocket, cutpurse	*naššēl*	نشّال
fraud, trickery	*náṣib* *iђtiyēl*	نصِب اِحْتِيال

to kill, murder	*ʔátal (yíʔtul)*	قتل (يِقْتُل)
murder	*ʔátil*	قتِل
murderer	*ʔētil*	قاتِل
swindler, con man	*naṣṣāb*	نصّاب
forger, counterfeiter	*muzáwwir*	مْزوِّر
forgery	*tazwīr*	تزْوير
bribe	*rášwi*	رشْوِة
kidnapping	*xáṭif*	خطِف
ransom	*fídyi*	فِدْيِة
court case	*ʔaḍíyyi (ʔaḍāya)*	قضية (قضايا)
interrogation	*taɧʔīʔ*	تحْقيق
court testimony	*idlēʔ bi-šhēdi*	إدْلاء بِشْهادِة
driver's license	*rúxṣit (ríxaṣ)* *dáftar swēʔa*	رُخْصِة (رِخص) سْواقة دفْتر سْواقة
penalty, fine	*mxālafi*	مْخالفِة
traffic ticket	*mxālafit sēr*	مْخالفِةْ سيرْ
fine	*ɣarāmi*	غرامِة
license suspension/ confiscation (as punishment)	*sáɧib rúxṣa* *sáɧib dáftar (isswēʔa)*	سحِب رُخْصة سحِب دفْتر (السّواقة)
traffic police	*šúrṭa -ssēr*	شُرْطِة السّيرْ
witness	*šēhid*	شاهِد

○

This lady tried to rob me.	*háydi -lmárra járrabit tisríʔni.*	هَيْدي المرّا جرّبِت تِسْرِقْني.
This man has changed his car's license plate number.	*háyda -zzálami mɣáyyir nímrit/ ráʔim siyyārtu.*	هَيْدا الزّلمي مْغيّر نِمرِةْ/رقِم سِيّارْتو.
I want to file an official complaint.	*báddi ʔáddim šákwa rasmíyyi.*	بدّي قدِّم شكْوَى رسْمية.
I want to report a nuisance.	*báddi á3mil máɧɖar 3an iz3āj.*	بدّي أعْمِل محْضر عن إزْعاج.
I want to report a nuisance.	*báddi bálliɣ 3an iz3āj.*	بدّي بلِّغ عن إزْعاج.
I want to report a big fight with gun shots.	*báddi bálliɣ 3an máškal kbīr fi ʔwāṣ.*	بدّي بلِّغ عن مشْكل كْبير في قْواص.
I want to follow up with the official complaint I made two months ago.	*báddi tēbi3 ilmáɧɖar yálli fatáɧtu min šahrēn.*	بدّي تابِع المحْضر يَلّي فتحْتو مِن شهْرين.

◇

You will be interrogated.	*raɧ titɧáwwal 3a-ttaɧʔīʔ.*	رح تِتْحوِّل عالتّحْقيق.
We're here to arrest ___.	*maʈlūb ilʔábiɖ 3a ___.*	مطْلوب القبِض عَ ___.
Photography is illegal in this area.	*mamnū3 ittaṣwīr hōn.*	ممْنوع التّصْوير هوْن.

Dealing with Difficulties

إذا في شي مِشْكْلِة

Lebanon is amazing in so many ways, but it can also be frustrating at times. But if you know what to expect, you'll be more equipped to deal with these frustrations with the least hassle. Some of the most common things you'll likely have to deal with include:

Lack of punctuality: Being late to everything, from meetings to social gatherings, is very typical in Lebanon. And, while it's not as habitual as it once was, it's still common enough that it warrants mention. In spite of this, it is not recommended to show up late to anything just because you think others might–because they may not, and you don't want to be the one who's disrespectful, unprofessional, or inappropriate (depending on the situation you find yourself in) by making people wait.

Nepotism: Nepotism is alive and well in Lebanon. You're unlikely to have to deal with it personally, unless you're in Lebanon long term or are there for professional reasons.

Bribes: Bribes are also still common practice in Lebanon, although not as much as they once were. These are typical in public institutions, when you're trying to obtain official documents. This corruption is becoming less and less acceptable, especially now that people are more likely to raise the issue and post on social media if they're asked to pay a bribe. As a foreigner, you're less likely to be asked for a bribe, as they know that, one, foreigners would find it unacceptable, and, two, foreigners are more likely to report bribery practices.

Lines/Queues: Standing in line used to be unheard of in Lebanon, and people would laugh and think you're nuts if you mentioned lines or reprimand someone for cutting in line. Things are much better now as more and more foreigners visit Lebanon, but, also, as more Lebanese travel abroad and expect people to respect lines.

Taking advantage of foreigners (financially): As a foreigner, you'll often be treated really kindly because you're a "guest" in the country, and people want to show you hospitality. That said, business owners, especially at markets where prices aren't set in stone, can be really welcoming and nice to you, but still give you the 'tourist prices' because they assume that you don't know better. Always ask that they give you the best price and don't be afraid to haggle; the worst that can happen is that they say no.

Language Barriers: People who know English will be respectful and try to speak English in front of you if they know that it's your mother tongue. Those who don't do this either don't know how to speak English or don't speak it well, or are trying to undermine you (especially in work environments), if they want to say something without you understanding. Do not be afraid to ask them to speak English, especially if it's a setting where you should know what is being said, because it's work-related, or it has to do with you personally.

Some of these and other situations are presented in the following dialogues.

Dealing with beggars

◇ وَلَوْ حيَلّا شي يا إسْتاذ.[1]
○ الله يْسهِّلَك.[2]
◇ والله مسْؤولِة عن أرْبع وْلاد، وبدّي أدْوية كِلّ شهِر بِخمْسين دوْلار.
○ الله يِشْفيكي ويِرْزْقِك.[2]

◇ I beg you, anything, sir.
○ May God make it easier for you.
◇ I'm responsible for four children, and my monthly medications cost $50.
○ May God heal you and provide for you.

◇ *waláw ɦayálla šī ya istēz.*[1]
○ *álla ysahhíllik.*[2]
◇ *wálla masʔūli 3an árba3 wlēd, w báddi ʔadwíyi kill šáhir bi-xamsīn dólar.*
○ *álla yišfīki w yírzʔik.*[2]

[1] عْطيني أيّ شي بْيِطْلع بِخاطْرك. *3ṭīni ayy šī byíṭla3 bi-xāṭrak.* **Give me anything to your liking.** (i.e. any amount you would like to give me, even if it is very little, I won't mind.)

[2] = الله معِك *álla má3ik* = الله يَعْطيكي *álla ya3ṭīki.* These four interchangeable expressions imply that you won't be giving any money and could translate as **sorry (but no)**.

2

DEALING WITH SOMEONE CUTTING IN LINE

- o سوْري بسّ دَوْري أنا.[1]
- ◇ أيْه بسّ إنْتي طْلِعْتي مْن الصّفّ وفلَّيْتي.
- o كِنْت بِالحمّام، وطلبِت مْن الشّخِص اللي كان واقِف وَرايي إنّو يِحْجِزْلي مطْرحي بِالصّفّ وما يْخلّي حدا ياخْدو.

- o Excuse me, it's my turn.
- ◇ But you stepped out of the line and walked away.
- o I was in the bathroom and I told the person standing behind me to hold my spot and not let anyone take it.

- o *[sorry] bass dáwri ána.*[1]
- ◇ *ē, bass ínti ṭlí3ti mn iṣṣáff w falláyti.*
- o *kínt bi-lħammēm, w ṭalábit mn iššáxiṣ -lli kēn wēʔif warāyi ínnu yiħjízli máṭraħi bi-ṣṣáff w ma yxálli ħáda yēxdu.*

[1] وِيْن رايِح و رامي حالك؟! دَوْري! *wēn rāyiħ w rēmi ħālak?! dáwri!* **What do you think you're doing?!** (lit. Where are you going and throwing yourself like that?!) **It's my turn!**

3

DEALING WITH HARASSMENT

◇ شو يا قشْطة؟[1]

o حْترِم حالك. إذا بِتْقرِّب أكْتر مِن هيْك، رح خلّيك تِنْدم.[2]

◇ شو، بْتِحْكي عربي كمان. شو رأْيك تِجي معي؟[3]

o رح تْحِلّ عنّي وتْخلِّص حالك؟ أَوْ بِحْسِب الله ما خلقك.[4]

◇ What's up, gorgeous!

o Behave yourself, and if you get any closer, you'll regret it.

◇ Wow, and you speak Arabic, too? How about you join me?

o Will you leave and save yourself or shall I make a scene here and make sure you go to hell?

◇ *šū ya ʔášṭa?*[1]

o *ḫtírim ḫālak. íza bitʔárrib áktar min hēk, raḫ xallīk tíndam.*[2]

◇ *šū, btíḫki 3árabi kamēn. šū ráʔyik tíji má3i?*[3]

o *raḫ tḫill 3ánni w txálliṣ ḫālak? aw bíḫsib álla ma xálaʔak.*[4]

[1] = شو يا حِلو؟ *šū ya ḫílu?*

[2] سْترْجي قرِّب *stárji ʔárrib* **Don't you dare come near me!**

[3] مِش قليلِة! *miš ʔalīli!* **You're feisty!** (lit. not minimal) مِش قليل! *miš ʔalīl!* is an expression used to address someone who has a strong personality or is surprisingly tough.

[4] رح تِخْرس أَوْ بْلِمّ عْليْك النّاس؟ *raḫ tíxras aw b-limm 3lēk innēs?* **Either you shut up or I'll draw attention.** (i.e. get everyone to gather around you)

○ سوْري بسّ أكْلي فيه رمِل بِقلْبو!
◇ مُسْتحيل[1] دُمْوازيْل. أكِلْنا كْتير مْنيح.
○ شو يَعْني أنا عم ألِّف؟[2]
◇ ما بعْرِف دُمْوازيْل، بسّ هَيْدي أوّل مرّة حدا بْيِشْتِكي عن أكِلْنا.
○ أوْكيْ، ما تزْعل بسّ إكْتُب عنْكُن عالسّوْشْيال ميدْيا.[3]

○ Excuse me, the food has some sand in it.
◇ No way, miss. Our food is perfectly good.
○ So, I'm making this up?!
◇ I don't know, miss, but this is the first time anyone has complained about our food.
○ Well, don't be upset when I post about you guys on social media!

○ *[sorry] bass ákli fī rámil bi-ʔálbu!*
◇ *mustaħīl[1], [Fdemoiselle]. akílna ktīr mnīħ.*
○ *šū yá3ni ána 3am állif?[2]*
◇ *ma bá3rif, [Fdemoiselle], bass háydi áwwal márra ħáda byištíki 3an ákilna.*
○ *okē, ma tíz3al bass íktub 3ánkun 3a-s[social media].*

[1] وَلا مُمْكِن *wála múmkin*

[2] = عم إخْترِع؟ *3am ixtírij;* عم كذِّب؟ *3am kázzib?* **Am I lying?**

[3] رح حِطِّلْكُم تِقْييم مِتْل الزِّفِت! *raħ ħiṭṭílkum tiʔyīm mitl izzífit!* **I'm going to give you a crappy rating!** (lit. like asphalt tar)

5

DEALING WITH AN PERSISTENT SALESPERSON

◇ ما بدّك تِشْتْري شي إسْتاذ؟

○ لأ، مرْسي.

◇ تعا تْفرّج وشوف. أسْعاري خَيالية.[1]

○ وَفّرِ عَ حالك حكي. منّي هوْن لإشْتْري.[2]

◇ Don't you want to buy anything, sir?

○ No, thanks.

◇ Just come and see for yourself. My prices are out of this world.

○ Save your breath. I'm not here to buy anyway.

◇ *ma báddak tíštri šī istēz?*

○ *la?, [Fmerci].*

◇ *tá3a tfárraj w šūf. as3āri xayēlíyyi.*[1]

○ *wáffir 3a ɧālak ɧáki. mánni hōn la-íštri.*[2]

[1] خِدْلك برْمِة! أسْعاري غيرْ شِكِل! *xídlak bármi! as3āri ɣēr šíkil!* **Take a look around! Our prices are unmatched!**

[2] حاج تْلِفّ وتْدُور! ما تْعزِّب حالك! **Stop trying. I'm not going to buy.** (lit. Enough turning and turning! Don't trouble yourself!)

6

Dealing with a salesperson who's trying to rip you off

○ قدّيْ هَيْدي پْليز؟[1]

◇ تِسْعين دوْلار.

○ ولَوْ! عم تِحْكي عن جدّ؟ عْطيني السِّعْر المظْبوط، مِش سِعْر السُّوّاح.[2]

◇ اه! هَيْقْتِك بْتعْرْفي خْبارْنا. مع إنّو لهْجْتِك ما كأنّا لِبْنانية. عَ كِلّ حال دْمْوازيْل، بسّ لِأنّو بْتِحْكي عربي مْنيح، دْفعي اللي بدِّك ياه.

○ How much is this, please?

◇ 90 dollars.

○ Oh, please! Are you serious? Give me the straight price, not the one for tourists.

◇ Oh! You seem to be familiar with our ways. But you don't sound like you're Lebanese. In any case, just because you speak Arabic so well, pay whatever you wish, Miss.

○ *ʔaddē háydi, [please]?*[1]

◇ *tis3īn dólar.*

○ *waláw! 3am tíḫki 3an jadd? 3ṭīni -ssí3r ilmaẓbūṭ, miš sí3r issuwwēḫ.*[2]

◇ *āh! háyʔtik btá3rfi xbārna. ma3 ínnu láhjtik ma ka-ánna libnēníyyi. 3a kill ḫāl, [Fdemoiselle], bass li-ánnu btíḫki 3árabi mnīḫ, dfá3i -lli báddik yēh.*

[1] = شو حقّا هَيْدي؟ *šū ḫáʔʔa háydi?*

[2] فاكِرْني هبْلِة؟ حاج تِسْتْلِمْني! *fēkírni hábli? ḫāj tistlímni!* **Do you think I'm stupid? Stop taking advantage of me!**

○ ضْبَيِة، پْليز.

◇ وَيْن عالمظْبوط بِضْبَيِة؟

○ أوْتيْل[1] لو رْوَيال.

◇ أوْكي طْلعي.

○ فيك تْدوِّر العدّاد؟

◇ الله يْصبّرِك يا روح![2]

○ سوْري؟[3]

◇ ما شي. ما عِنّا عدّادات هوْن.

○ أوْكي. قدّيْ بدّك تاخُد مِنّي مِن هوْن لهونيك؟

◇ خلّينا نمِشي بِالأوّل، مْنرِجع مْنِحْكي. وَلا يْهِمِّك.[4]

○ أوْكي. طيِّب.

(The taxi approaches the hotel.)

○ بِنْزل هوْن پْليز.

◇ مِتِل ما بدِّك مادام.[5]

○ قدّيْ بِتْريد[6] مْعلِّم؟

◇ خلِّيا عْلَيْنا هَيْدي المرّة.

○ مرْسي كْتير. قدّيْ بِتْريد؟

◇ عِشْرين ألْف ليرة.

○ كيف عِشْرين ألْف؟ مْفكّرْني ما بعْرِف تِسْعيرات التّاكْسي؟

◇ عِشْرين ألْف. فيكي تِطْلعي وتِسْألي حَيْلّا تاكْسي مارِق.[7]

○ هَيْدا المِشْوار مِش أكْتر مِن[8] عشِرْتلاف.

◇ عشِرْتلاف شو مدام؟ أيّا سِنِة عايْشِة إنْتي؟[9]

○ طيِّب، رح تاخِدا؟ أَوْ منروح عِنْد الشُّرْطة ومْنِسْألُن.

◇ ما تْهدِّديني مدام. أنا الحقّ عْلَيي وَقّفْتِلِّك[10].

o أوْكيْ، عظيم. هَوْدي مِصْرياتك عالمقْعد وَرا. كفّي حكي وَحْدك.

o Dbayeh, please.

◇ Where exactly in Dbayeh?

o Le Royal hotel.

◇ Okay, get in.

o Would you please turn on the meter?

◇ Oh, jeez!

o Excuse me?

◇ Nothing... we don't have meters here.

o Okay, how much will you charge me from here to there?

◇ Let's start moving first, lady, and then we'll see. Don't worry.

o Very well then.

(The taxi approaches the hotel.)

o I'll get out here, please.

◇ As you wish, ma'am.

o How much is the fare, sir?

◇ Leave it on us this time!

o Thanks a lot... how much is it, please?

◇ 20,000 L.L.

o How is it 20,000 L.L.? You think I don't know fares?

◇ It's 20,000 L.L., and you can get out and ask any taxi passing by.

o This trip should cost no more than 10,000 L.L.!

◇ 10,000 what, woman?! What year are you from?

o All right, will you take it or shall we go to the police station and ask them?

◇ Don't you dare threaten me, ma'am. My mistake was that I stopped and picked you up.

o Okay, great... Here's your money on the back seat. Continue the conversation by yourself.

○ *ḍbáyi, [please].*
◇ *wēn 3a-lmaẓbūṭ bi-ḍbáyi?*
○ *[[F]hôtel][1] [[F]Le Royal].*
◇ *okē ṭlá3i.*
○ *fīk tdáwwir il3addēd?*
◇ *álla yṣábbrik ya rūḫ![2]*
○ *[sorry]?[3]*
◇ *ma šī. ma 3ínna 3addēdēt hōn.*
○ *okē. ʔaddē báddak tēxud mínni min hōn la-hunīk?*
◇ *xallīna nímši bi-lʔáwwal, mnírja3 mníḫki. wála yhímmik.[4]*
○ *okē. ṭáyyib.*

(The taxi approaches the hotel.)

○ *bínzal hōn, [please].*
◇ *mítil ma báddik, [[F]madame].[5]*
○ *ʔaddē bitrīd[6] m3állim?*
◇ *xallíya 3láyna háydi -lmárra.*
○ *[[F]merci] ktīr. ʔaddē bitrīd?*
◇ *3išrīn alf līra.*
○ *kīf 3išrīn alf? mfakkárni ma bá3rif tis3īrāt ittáksi?*
◇ *3išrīn alf. fīki tiṭlá3i w tisʔáli ḫayálla táksi mēri?.[7]*
○ *háyda -lmišwār miš áktar min[8] 3aširtalēf.*
◇ *3aširtalēf šū, [[F]madame]? áyya síni 3āyši ínti?[9]*
○ *ṭáyyib, raḫ tēxida? aw minrūḫ 3ind iššúrṭa w mnisʔálun.*
◇ *ma thaddidīni, [[F]madame]. ána -lḫaʔʔ 3láyi waʔʔaftíllik[10].*
○ *okē, 3aẓīm. háwdi miṣriyētak 3a-lmáʔ3ad wára. káffi ḫáki wáḫdak.*

1 = فُنْدُق *fúnduʔ*

2 = اسْتغْفرَ الله العظيم! *stáɣfara -llāh il3aẓīm!*

3 = عفْواً؟ *3áfwan?*; شو؟ *šū?* **What?**

4 ما تِعْتَلي همّ. بسّ نوصل مْنِحْكي. *ma tí3tali hamm. bass nūṣal, mníḫki.* **Don't worry. When we arrive, we'll discuss it.**

5 = مِتِل ما بِتْريدي. *mítil ma bitrīdi.*

6 = قدّيْ بْتِؤْمُر؟ *ʔaddē btíʔmur?*

7 سْألي أيّ حدا! هَيْدي التّسْعيرة! *sʔáli ayy ḫáda! háydi -ttis3īra!*

8 = ما بيكلّف أكْتر مِن *ma bikállif áktar min*

[9] وين مْفكْرة حالِك؟ *wēn mfákkra Ħālik?* **Where do you think you are?**; عَ أيّ كَوْكب عايْشِة؟ *3a ayy káwkab 3āyša?* **What planet do you live on?**

[10] = طلّعْتِك *ţallá3tik*

Vocabulary

to verbally harass, catcall	*tá??al (ytá??il) damm/bi-lħáki námmar (ynámmir)*	تقّل (يْتقِّل) دمّ/بِالحكي نمّر (يْنمِّر)
verbal harassment	*tinmīr tí?il damm*	تِنْمير تِقِل دمّ
to sexually harass someone	*tħárraš (yitħárraš)*	تْحرّش (يِتْحرّش)
sexual harassment	*taħárruš jínsi*	تحرُّش جِنْسي
to push	*dáfaš (yídfuš)*	دفش (يِدْفُش)
to bother, annoy, provoke, harass	*zá3aj (yíz3ij), tħárkaš (yitħárkaš) fī*	زعج (يِزْعِج) تْحرْكش (يِتْحرْكش) في
lack of manners, crudeness	*?íllit ádab/ axlē?/tihzīb*	قِلّةْ أدب/ أخْلاق/تِهْذيب
bad service	*xídmi 3āţli*	خِدْمِة عاطْلِة
to report	*bállaɣ (ybálliɣ)*	بلّغ (يْبلِّغ)
report	*balēɣ*	بلاغ
complaint	*šákwa (šakēwi)*	شكْوى (شكاوي)
to scream, cry out	*şárax (yíşrux)*	صرخ (يِصْرُخ)
situation	*máw?af (mawē?if) wáđi3 (awđā3)*	مَوْقف (مَواقِف) وَضِع (أَوْضاع)
accident	*ħādis*	حادِث

fight, argument	*xnēʔa* *máškal*	خْناقة مشْكل
beggar	*šaђђād*	شحّاد

Expressions

O

Help!	*ilђaʔūni!* *sē3dūni!*	اِلْحقوني! ساعْدوني!
Thief!	*ђarāmi!*	حرامي!
Behave yourself!	*ђtírim ђālak!*	حْترِم حالك!
Shame on you!	*3ēb 3lēk!*	عيْب عليْك!
Shame on you, at your age!	*3ēb 3lēk, ḑī3ān kábirtak!* *3ēb 3lēk, stíђi 3a šáybtak!*	عيْب علْيك، ضِيعان كبرِْتك! عيْب علْيك، سْتِحي عَ شَيْبْتك!
That man over there is bothering us.	*háyda -zzálami -lli hunīk 3am yiz3íjna.*	هَيْدا الزّلمي اللي هونيك عم يِزْعِجْنا.
I want to report a case of sexual harassment.	*báddi bálliɣ 3an ђādsit taђárruš jínsi.*	بدّي بلِّغ عن حادْثِةْ تحرُّش جِنْسي.
Someone is following and verbally harassing us.	*ђáda lēђiʔna w 3am yitђárkaš fīna.*	حدا لاحِقْنا وعم يِتْحرْكش فينا.
It's been a month, and my papers have yet to be issued.	*wrāʔi ṣárlun šáhir w ba3d ma xílṣu.*	وْراقي صرْلْن شهِر وبعْد ما خِلْصوا.

I've been standing in line forever.	*ṣárli wáʔit wēʔif bi-ṣṣáff.*	صرْلي وَقِت واقِف بِالصفّ.
Excuse me, can you make some room (for me to pass)?	*[sorry], fīk tmarrʔíni/tʔaṭṭí3ni?*	سوْري، فيك تْمرّقِني/تْقطِّعْني؟
Hey! Look where you're going!	*hēy hēy! tṭálla3 wēn rāyiḫ!* *hēyhēy! tṭálla3 ʔiddēmak ínta w mēši!*	هاي هاي! تْطلّع ويْن رايِح! هاي هاي! تْطلّع قِدّامك إنْتَ وماشي!
(to a taxi driver) You're taking us for a long ride when the trip is actually short!	*axádna 3a ṭarīʔ ṭawīl, bass mišwārna kēn mafrūḍ ykūn ʔaṣīr.*	آخدْنا عَ طريق طَويل، بسّ مِشْوارْنا كان مفْروض يْكون قصير.
We're not stupid. Are you going to give us reasonable prices or shall we leave?	*mánna mjēdīb/ mahēbīl/masāṭīl, raḫ ta3ṭīna sí3ir mítl ilxáliʔ/maʔbūl, aw minfíll?*	منّا مْجاديب/ مباهيل/مساطيل، رح تعْطينا سِعِر مِتْل الخلِق/مقْبول، أَوْ منْفِلّ؟

www.ingramcontent.com/pod-product-compliance
Lightning Source LLC
Chambersburg PA
CBHW052055110526
44591CB00013B/2213
* 9 7 8 1 9 4 9 6 5 0 0 7 5 *